WOMANSONG

WOMANSONG
Balance & Harmony in a Feminine Key

Gwen Suesse

Sumi Brush Calligraphy and Watercolor
By Renée Locks

Sing your song with Joy!

Namaste —
Gwen Suesse

Watercolor and Calligraphy: Renée Locks

PERMISSIONS GRANTED

Excerpt from **The Book of Awakening** by Mark Nepo with permission of Conari Press,
imprint of Red Wheel/Weiser. 1-800-423-7087 www.redwheelweiser.com

From *They're Playing Your Song* by Alan Cohen as published in his *From the Heart* column.
Used by permission. All rights reserved. For more information on Alan Cohen's books and programs,
visit www.alancohen.com

Quotation by Dr. Elisabeth Kübler-Ross. Used by permission of the
Elisabeth Kübler-Ross Foundation.

The book was produced by

Sea-Hill Press, Inc.
P.O. Box 60301
Santa Barbara, CA 93160
Production Manager: Greg Sharp
Design & Layout: Judy Petry
Copyeditor: Cynthia Sharp

www.seahillpress.com
Printed in Hong Kong

ISBN: 978-0-615-33104-1

Dedication

From generation to generation,
The music of life continues…

In loving memory of my mother,
Louise Fellows von der Osten
(1906–2004)

Ever gracious, generous, wise—
An inspiration to all who knew her.

And for my children,
Jennifer and Ned

Carrying the melodies to
new places in new keys…

Contents

What Is Woman?

Beyond all the roles
daughter, friend, lover, wife, mother, worker, homemaker
is there some way,
some space,
for her to be her own person?
Surely, surely, there's a way.
It's a matter of finding a framework,
a feminine way to balance these roles
and allow the emergence of
Harmony.

Prelude

Properly, a piece of music
designed to be played as an introduction
to another composition.

If seeds in the dark earth
can turn into such beautiful flowers,
what can the heart of a woman
become
in her long journey to the stars.

adapted, G.K. Chesterton

The Many
and Varied Melodies
of Woman

Song sung blue
Everybody knows one.
—NEIL DIAMOND

Indeed, we all know about the blues, but there are other songs within us, many and varied. The quest to be ourselves is long and is marked by both cacophony and utter silence. The Sirens, however, our true voices, are singing within, singing without ceasing, melodiously calling to us, patiently awaiting our discovery of them. We need only hear them, listen to them, and learn to sing along. And so, let the musical journey begin.

A prelude is a musical piece designed to introduce, to set a mood. In these pages, I invite you to break into the pandemonium of contemporary life and take a thoughtful detour through the imagery of music. Music, immeasurable, ineffable, can lead you to discoveries that lie within you, waiting to be noticed. Let us pause and deliberately suspend our everyday exigencies. Let us transport ourselves to a realm of images that is conducive to introspection and reflection.

Womansong reflects on the stages, circumstances, and conundrums of being a woman. All of us, God willing, will experience all the stages of womanhood. And however old we are, we don't lose the earlier ages, we just add on the new ones; the fragments of our old songs fuse with new riffs as they emerge. While the journey I describe is a very personal one, I believe the resulting illuminations are universally useful, something to be shared with other women.

Although *Womansong* is a book for women of all ages and circumstances, it is first and foremost an invitation to mothers and daughters to begin a conversation. How complicated are the relationships between we mothers and we daughters! Many of us are filling both roles at the same time, and the competing demands and complex interactions among generations are unsettling to our equilibrium. At one moment, we are competent professionals who enjoy the respect of our workplace colleagues; at the next, an incoming phone call can instantly transform us into deferential daughters, struggling to find ways to listen to Mom without feeling obligated to do what she says, or worse, what she implies.

At another point in our lives, we may be arbitrating an argument between our children in an authoritative manner while concurrently caught in the poignant, painful task of negotiating with aging parents who resist making necessary lifestyle changes. It's as if we wear hats with multiple corners and yank them around speedily so that the appropriate label—and persona—is front and center: Mother, Daughter, and sometimes, hopefully, Me.

Add to this mix the baggage of past experiences, the press of present commitments and responsibilities, and the still, small voices of our true selves that persistently seek to be heard, and it's no wonder that the tapestries we weave of our lives are wild, untamed creations. Our designs-in-progress weave together strands of pride, loyalty, respect, and love so fierce that it hurts, along with darker threads from our shadow sides, those parts we'd rather ignore or deny, dicey things like competition, jealousy, and the need to be right and oh so separate.

As a daughter, I look back and remember my mother's advice on allergy medicine. Was I interested? No, thank you! In spite of Mother's life-long battle with allergies and finding what worked, I had my own ideas about how I would deal with this challenge. As a mother, I think of my own daughter, determined to sweep back her bangs for her fourth-grade school picture. She brought home Most Unbecoming Pictures. I remember trying to figure out what I could possibly say about those photos. This is one of our funny, mother-daughter memories. Jennifer was worried that I'd be angry with her for re-doing her hair; I was just trying to find some way to comment without hurting her feelings. Oddly, it is my fourth-grade picture that my big sister uses to this day to embarrass me. Sisters, mothers, daughters—the threads of identity, competition, and conflicts repeat themselves again and again, from generation to generation. Mercifully, love and familial bonds are tenacious, and persevere in spite of all manner of calamities and challenges.

In an intricate *contredanse*, we seek our unique, individual identities. At times we are aligned with and moving in tandem with the beloved women in our lives. At other times, we parry, executing dizzying pirouettes with the enthusiastic exclamations of prima ballerinas whose movements seem to say, "Look at me! I am unique!" We look at our mothers and evaluate (to use a much kinder verb than judge) their choices as a means of making our own. We struggle to find that magical place where we can love them, like them, emulate them, and repudiate them, all in the same place and at the same time. No wonder the goal eludes us.

Intuitively, I suspect that the path to balance and harmony in our individual feminine lives lies beyond the mother-daughter themes, where painful memories muddle with good ones and confound our efforts to be whole. We can get beyond these themes and into personal integration by listening to each other, by having the courage to examine our histories, and by honoring and celebrating our differences as well as our similarities. Like solving a life-long riddle, we weave, unravel, and re-weave, searching for that centered place where we can bring into balance the best of like/not like, for balance, as always, is the key to harmony.

Here we are, then, a motley assortment of mothers, daughters, sisters, and friends, united by biology while separated by our unique personalities and circumstances. Some of us are married, some single, some divorced, and some widowed. We are young, middle-aged, or in the autumn of life. We are quiet or gregarious, studious or action-oriented. The variations are many, yet our commonalities are significant.

Whatever our situations, from underneath all our cannot-be-denied obligations, a voice whispers to us, almost imperceptibly. A voice asks us where we are hiding our carefree abandon, our joy, and our creative energy. A voice urges us to restore balance and harmony; it calls us to re-examine our lives gently and lovingly. A voice dares us to be proactive, grab the reins, and stop letting life happen to us.

Significantly, it doesn't seem to matter what circumstances describe us, for the feminine experience is universal. We yearn for meaning. We long for wholeness. We crave balance. We seek to nurture ourselves and those people and things that are important to us. And although the circumstances and timing may vary, the same questions come to us all.

What's new here? What resolution does *Womansong* offer?

Ultimately, only personal discovery makes things "new." A woman's life is a journey of questions. The German lyric poet Rainer Maria Rilke tells us that we need to "learn to live the questions." Mothers and daughters, sisters and aunts, women of all ages, nationalities, circumstances, and callings share a kinship of biology that presents some universal questions. In some ways, nothing much has changed in spite of society's struggles over the past century. Through the generations, we've tried different solutions, always in a quest for personal and societal answers. While each generation thinks it is different and has finally figured "it" out, questions continue to arise. Certainly, that has been true of the quest for equality in the workplace. In a never-ending cycle, the "answers" of one generation spawn a new set of questions for the next.

Our individual journeys take on different outward appearances, yet striking similarities remain, regardless of what generation we represent. Underneath whirling societal evolution, the yearning for wholeness is the bedrock. Ultimately, every one of us is trying to figure out how to take what we've been given and somehow incorporate our innate sense of who we are within that structure.

The winds of change blow unceasingly across the continents of our social paradigms. Sometimes change is a soft, warm breeze; sometimes it is a hurricane-force microburst that changes our coastlines with cataclysmic speed. Women just go on. We cope, we adapt, we commiserate, and we hang on tenaciously. When we are undermined with doubts, however, our ability to cope gracefully and with compassion is sorely tried. *Womansong* seeks to cast light on these doubts and to help mothers and daughters understand each other's outlooks. Whether our musings are solos or duets, *Womansong* gives us language and ideas to tether our communications to the realm of trust and respect. As the pages go by, I hope you will find yourself humming along, your song reflecting your inner music effortlessly and with joy.

> *Sometimes one must travel far*
> *to discover what is near.*
> —URI SHULEVITZ

Now I become myself. It's taken
Time, many years and places;
I have been dissolved and shaken,
Worn other people's faces...

MAY SARTON

Musical Forms

The general principles
and schemes which govern
the structure-at-large of
a composition.

How This Musical Journey Is Organized

It doesn't happen all at once...
You become. It takes a long time.
—MARGERY WILLIAMS

Womansong's medley of metaphors, illustrations, quotes, essays, and remembered experiences brings together a unique mix of thoughts about self-awareness, spirituality, art, and social research, with the whole equaling more than the sum of its parts. Perhaps unremarkable as separate snippets, when combined, these elements inspire illuminations, suggest alternatives, and offer glimmers of the possibility of achieving balance and serenity.

When I began writing, personal discovery was my goal. I was searching to understand my feelings and to find positive ways to channel my energies within my circumstances. I'd been told to give the first-draft stage free rein in order to see where intuition led. After a few arduous, blind starts, my writing seemed to take off on a course of its own. Unbidden, the "voice" I didn't know I was seeking emerged. I found myself in a peculiar, singular groove, not so much a "writer" as a conduit responding to forces outside, or perhaps within, myself. Thoughts jumped onto the page, surprising me as much as they may ultimately surprise my readers.

After finishing the first draft, I looked at it all and said, "Now what?

How can I structure these essays into a cohesive whole and give them a comprehensible form?" Curiously, I found myself thinking in terms of musical metaphors. Initially, this intuitive leap surprised me, but it shouldn't have. We think in terms of what we know. My early professional training was in music; therefore, it was natural that my struggles as a woman would define themselves in musical terms. The definitions of musical terms are surprisingly apt when applied to a woman's journey through life.

In music, our ears long for patterns, for something we can recognize and hold on to, hum along with, or sing when we are in the shower. Over the history of music, various forms developed. These were prescribed formats for making sense of pitches, rhythms, timbres, melodies, and harmonies. These forms impose order and a comprehensible design, giving listeners a comfortable starting point, a familiarity that allows them to relax and listen. It is fascinating that this happens on a non-verbal level. Relatively few people have learned about specific musical forms, yet most people know when a composition works, simply because it speaks to them.

Thus began a surge of thoughts that ultimately took on a life of its own. I pored over the *Harvard Dictionary of Music*, fascinated by how many musical terms also could be used to describe life situations. Counterpoint: multiple melodies vying for attention and importance, just like the various factors in a busy woman's life. Interludes: insertions, not unlike life's interruptions. Leitmotifs: dominant and recurring themes. Apparently life and music have a lot in common!

I pondered life's mixed messages as if they were voices in a choir. How encouraging: the rich sonorities of a choir, finely tuned, produce an effect far greater than the sum of its parts. Might it be that my inner voices, singing together, could also be more powerful and more beautiful if I could wrestle them into harmony?

Of course, in reality, it's not that simple. The challenge is to figure out how to sort out the nebulous voices, how to distinguish the "real" parts from the many layers piled on by socialization, culture, society's demands, and Mother Necessity. How can we extract them from the choir, one part at a time, look at them, listen to them, and examine them for what they really mean in the most personal way? How can we alter these voices in order to encourage symbiotic relationships, much as an orchestra tunes up before a performance?

"Who is writing this book?" asked an editor. "Is it the musician/artist, or is it the teacher?" It happens that this musician/artist was a teacher, and somehow you never get the teacher out of a person. It's a way of being. Still, the question remains: Why do these two distinct personalities seem to tag-team as they make appearances throughout my writing? It's no idle coincidence that research and objectivity keep intruding on questions of the heart. Without the greater objectivity garnered from sociologists, theologians, novelists, philosophers, and other sources, one risks living in a dream world, or dangling on the precipice of despair, unable to see alternatives, possibilities, and hope.

In the opening of *Bright Flows the River*, novelist Taylor Caldwell writes, "In the dark night of the soul, bright flows the river of God." She tells her story as seen through the eyes of a strong, independent woman who knows how to assert herself. In her words I found encouragement during my own dark night of the soul to speak up for myself. Reading Frank Sulloway's *Born to Rebel*, I gleaned a new and much-needed understanding of the effects of birth order on family dynamics and personal development, which helps me deal with the often-irrational interactions between family members.

Over time, as discoveries piggyback on one another, we come to realize that emotional health depends on the balance between heart and mind. The sages have long told us this, of course, but truly comprehending this personally, for ourselves, is a significant turning point on the road to wholeness. A sense of well-being depends on both spheres. Art, poetry, and music take us beyond the ordinary; they help us to dream. Objectivity, logic, and research ground us in reality. Balance. It always comes back to balance. Balance is achieved not only through direct experiences, but also from bits and pieces gathered, like a collection of shells to study and treasure, from novels, self-help books, sociology, psychology, spiritual readings, and women's studies. These readings provide the insights that comfort us. They give us the strength to forge ahead. The artist alone would have withered years ago. It is the teacher who empowers the artist to bloom with intentionality.

Thinking about quoting these rich sources led to another quandary: Would quotes dilute what I had to say? Did I not trust my own thoughts? In the end, the decision to include quotes was an easy one: Many times, one magic sentence from something I've read or heard has replaced hours of meandering thought, capturing the essence of a concept I've been struggling to articulate with incandescent clarity. Talismans are meant to be shared!

Another stylistic thread which comes out in my writing is an emphasis on defining specific words. This is a gift from my mother, who taught me from toddlerhood to love and to question words. My family always had an unabridged dictionary within reach, so we learned to appreciate precision and nuance in our choice of words. This habit stuck with me. It is astonishing, at times, to look up a common word with a commonly understood definition only to find something more: a shading, perhaps; a possibility or a limitation that changes the way you see that word's essence. When I'm stuck, it is often *The American Heritage Dictionary* that gets me moving once again.

What I have just described are design threads. There is a "thread of the spirit," as well, which comes from an epiphany that emerged as I started writing: I realized with sudden clarity that the defining core of my search has been my inability to accept the duality of joy and sorrow. I spent years proclaiming only the positive aspects of my experiences, subconsciously afraid that admitting the negatives would somehow obliterate what has been good. How could I talk about the frustrations of squirming adolescents in my school classroom without sounding like an immature, spoiled brat myself? How could I discuss the tedium of dealing with the Terrible Two's without implying that I resented my babies? How could I complain about little peccadilloes without risking my image as a sunny, can-do person?

This tendency has a different quality in younger women. Enviably, they seem far more able than my generation was to stand up for themselves, especially in the professional realm. Yet the vulnerability of younger women seems to seep out in other areas, as they, like those of us born in an earlier time, struggle to embrace the paradoxes of negatives inextricably tied to positives. These issues, alas, only magnify when they are considered forbidden topics to be kept to oneself. While our awareness of this challenge is not always conscious, while we may have trouble articulating it, when one woman mentions difficulties with facing negatives, other women smile and shake their heads with quiet, knowing compassion. We've all been there, it seems.

Perhaps we aren't sure the negative sides, the frustrations and the disappointments of our journeys, will hold up to scrutiny. We want, oh so very ardently, for our choices to be the right choices. What if they aren't? We push and cram those niggling doubts into a corner, build walls of proclaimed benefits and advantages around them, and do our best to be indefatigably positive and invincible.

Truth will not be held at bay indefinitely. The truth is that benefits and drawbacks will ever be bedfellows, coexisting no matter what efforts we exert to the contrary.

When I was sixteen years old, I was given a copy of Kahlil Gibran's *The Prophet*. For forty years, my favorite chapter has been "Joy and Sorrow." Gibran is clear: "Your joy is your sorrow unmasked." He goes on to explain that the very things that bring us happiness are rooted also in heartaches. Not only are these qualities inextricably bound together, but further, "the deeper that sorrow carves into your being, the more joy you can contain."

How ironic that my favorite chapter would be a message that short-circuited. It never made the leap from intellectual concept to the inner truth I badly needed so that I could put the pieces of my life together. Perhaps that particular passage was a favorite because my heart knew that it needed to be front and center until I finally "got it."

Well! I get it. When I am troubled, when experiences are painful, I need to remember I am experiencing the dark side of the moon. If I persevere, accepting bad with good and downs as well as ups, light will re-emerge. But this will happen only if am willing to go through the depths rather than deny them.

Bit by agonizing bit, I have found my way to a good place, a place where I can appreciate the gifts of womanhood in spite of the sacrifices women make in today's society. This is the book I would have loved to find on a shelf twenty years ago, a book that would have helped me know that my struggles were not unique, and more important, not hopeless. It is my hope that *Womansong*'s musical imagery and reflections articulate how social issues and questions of our time may be coaxed into insights and possibilities as we "work them over" like dedicated composers, unafraid of trying new things and "re-writing" the sections that aren't working. Our reward for keeping our eyes and ears open to harmony wherever it shyly, but surely, may be residing will be emerging resolutions and a measure of serenity.

God's grace, loving family, and friends have lit my way. May your journey be so blessed, as well.

Conductor

The basic function of the conductor is to interpret the music for the group.

Beyond myself
Somewhere
I wait for
my arrival.

OCTAVIO PAZ

The Long, Convoluted Journey to the Present

When you begin your education, you often have little idea where it will lead. So it was with me. I wanted to be a teacher—how typical of my generation of women—but I had no idea what I would teach. From childhood on, however, choral singing has always been one of my most favorite things. Things happen when people sing together, non-verbal things that are hard to describe but oh so very powerful. There are times when the singers are so aligned with the music and with each other that it feels like electric energy is running through the chorus. I have experienced occasions when sixty voices effortlessly act as one, "thinking" together, twisting a phrase in a new way together, without having discussed or planned it beforehand. These sorts of experiences hooked me, and I gravitated to directing choirs as if pulled by a strong magnet.

Conductors choose musical pieces and are responsible for interpreting them. Their job is to make the music's meaning comprehensible to the audience, as well as to the singers. Bringing music to life is an intuitive process that involves imagery, technique, passion, and more than a little luck.

As we embark on this metaphorical musical journey together, it may be helpful to get acquainted with the conductor. Who am I? What colors my thinking? What experiences have formed the "melodies" that make up my life, and how have they affected my quest for harmony and balance?

My grand entrance occurred on May 31, 1945, as a weary nation awaited the end of a long, horrible war. My ambivalence about women's issues, work, and family may stem from the fact that I was a "cusp baby," born just as one era ended and another began, with one foot in the old order and one in the new.

I was a late-life surprise, born to parents who had post-Victorian values and ideas. I grew up with a social ethos that vaporized in the turbulence of the sixties, just as I came into adulthood. This created a curious dichotomy, a struggle between the social sensibility of the fifties and the emergent women's rights movement. I grew up expected to defer to men, a message I received not only from the patriarchal fifties' model, but also from the unspoken but powerful example set by my lovely mother, who arranged her life around my father. I chose my career because it was open to women, never questioning why I couldn't choose what I really wanted to do. Then, suddenly, in the social anarchy of the sixties, I was expected to defer to no one. In my mother's generation, women who stayed home to raise their children were honored; by the time I was in my twenties, they were scorned, or perhaps worse, simply ignored and overlooked.

My childhood was standard, middle-class, WASP ordinary, which is to say that it was blessed beyond measure. I lived with both parents and three siblings. We were warm, safe, and well cared for. I was educated in a small rural school where everyone knew everyone else. It was safe to roam the neighborhood and explore wherever I pleased. My parents were cultured people who cared about manners, politics, and the larger world.

I emerged from childhood with two priceless gifts from them: first, I was loved unconditionally; second—and remarkably, given my father's aristocratic, Old-World background—females were treated the same as males in my family. My parents assumed that I deserved an education just as much as my brother did. They were determined that all their children, male and female, would learn to take care of themselves. This heritage of independence and self-worth influenced my decisions and buoyed me up during many dark, doubting moments.

I went to college in suburban New York City, quite a change for a country girl. I soaked in all the city advantages I could, attending concerts, visiting museums, and treasuring new friendships with students from all over the country. Those were heady, broadening times. I remember precisely—in the most palpable, physical way—my extraordinary feeling of freedom and independence. I woke up every day and inhaled a deep breath of the world being mine to grab, shape, and conquer! Achieving success was never in question.

Off I went into the wide world to find my fortune. Had the option seemed open to me, I would have become a minister. Ministry combined so many of my passions and values: spirituality, music, faith, beauty, helping others, writing, speaking, and community; all these combined in an indescribable mystic communion. Instead, lured by a fabulous college choir experience into majoring in music, I became a choral music teacher. The podium became my pulpit, a place to express my belief that the arts can help humankind to understand one another and replace ignorance and hostility with enlightenment and kindness.

I loved teaching—not for the schools themselves, but the students, the young people who challenged my thinking and responded to my respect for them. Even so, it was a lonely, incomplete time. Although I had chosen to be a happy, high-functioning person, I continued to feel like I didn't quite "fit." Maybe that's not unusual; I don't know. As an adolescent, I was too smart. At the head of my class in a very small rural school, I felt I was viewed as some sort of quirky, benign egghead to be consulted about all my classmates' dating problems but never having dates myself. In college, I was too independent; I found sororities untenable, stigmatizing, and stultifying, an attitude through which, ultimately, I defined yet another lonely course for myself. As a new teacher, my vision of education differed radically from the entrenched norm. I was young, eager, idealistic, and appalled by the mediocrity I saw in public schools, where enthusiastic young minds were stuffed and stultified into tidy categories, standards, and classroom logistics.

I was also lonely once again and full of niggling suspicions that something must be wrong with me. I had friends and work I loved, but no partner to ground me. I longed to share with a special man the everyday, the sublime, and everything in between.

And then came Jack, my husband, like water in the desert or light in a dark cave. He reflected my better self, allowing the values, dreams, purpose, and laughter trapped inside me to emerge and flourish, fed by his love and enthusiasm. He appeared, as is often the case, when I least expected him. I had given up on ever finding a compatible partner. I was quite busy, thank you very much, with teaching and vocal coaching. And then one day, there he was, standing behind a stage curtain, full of good humor, eyes dancing, asking me to hold a flashlight while he adjusted the theater lights. My mother had always said I'd "know" when the right man came along. Indeed! We married six weeks after our first date.

Oh, I can hear the objections of the sixties' extreme feminist point of view even now, throwing up at the thought that a woman's growth could only occur through a man's love. That was my experience, although I am sure there can be other paths to that same growth. There were parts of me that could not bloom without the light from another's soul. Someone needed to believe in me so that I could believe in myself. Until that point, there was the world, and then there was me, feeling like an anomaly, an aberration.

Suddenly, I had new energy. Jack's enthusiasm was contagious. He thought I was neat and funny—maybe I actually was neat and funny! Jack, who was also involved in the fine arts as a technical theater professional, understood my passion for music. Very much his own man, a putterer and builder at heart, he was comfortable giving me lots of space. I thrived in such a supportive environment; I felt free to grow, to do, to experiment, to think, and I was refreshed and heartened by our easy compatibility.

Marriage brought with it a new set of identity challenges. How could I reconcile my former style of independent decision-making with my new status as a wife, including another person's needs, desires, and preferences along with my own? How would we set priorities? Whose Christmas traditions would we follow? Jack's family hid presents until Christmas Eve. I felt that wrapped presents were works of art to look at, anticipate, and enjoy for days, if not weeks, ahead of time. What happens when we don't want the same things, when he wants a boat and she wants new carpet?

Early marriage was a whirlwind of discoveries: learning male rhythms and male logic, God love them, so different from ours; designing and building a house, and I do mean building, even though I'd never before hammered a nail; moving to a new community with all the energy that takes; making new friends; changing jobs. It was a wild and crazy but entirely energizing time in my life. As a teacher, I was blessed with regular time off, time to think, to read, and to grow personally as well as professionally. These regular breaks from the hectic world of teaching were pro-foundly helpful. I don't know how most people manage with only a week or two a year to re-group, rest, relax, and vacation.

With motherhood came sublime rewards and fierce trials. No woman can begin to imagine the magnitude of feelings, bonding, and responsi-bility she will feel for the baby she has experienced within her and then, miraculously, holds in her arms. Suddenly, all the old priorities and old modes of operation are obsolete. I had no idea how all-encompassing these changes would be. Like many other women, I had only a vague vision of how we would fit a baby into our lives. It was a tidy vision, though: crib, toys, highchair, and lullabies. I didn't know how tired I'd be. How over-whelmed. How little I'd "accomplish." I was supremely happy with my baby daughter, but already nervous about losing my fledgling, emerging self.

Thus began a long roller coaster ride, full of dazzling highs but also frightening lows. We had chosen to live in a remote country setting, influ-enced, I suppose, by the "back to nature" sensibility of the Hippie Sixties. We learned to live in harmony with the seasons: gardening, preserving bounty, cutting firewood, and snuggling by the woodstove on cold win-ter nights. We strove for simplicity and self-reliance. Gradually, we made friends in our new community. Those were good times, but from deep inside came insistent murmurs, murmurs that didn't fit the picture, mur-murs about identity, about "meaningful" work, about roles, destiny, and evaporating time.

These voices, murmurs, dreams, and ideas crystallized into tangible form when I was thirty-eight years old, prompted by Gail Sheehy's *Path-finders*, which is subtitled *Overcoming the Crises of Adult Life and Finding Your Own Path to Well-Being*. I had already read *Passages*, her book outlin-ing adult development. This follow-up book described the "winners," men and women who leapt from the pages with vitality and creative solutions to life's problems and challenges. Although I never used the word out loud, this book prompted a full-fledged crisis. I did not see myself anywhere in those pages of winners, even though excellence in any endeavor had always been my goal. I spoke of this to no one, not even to my beloved husband, who was also my best friend. The specter of failure, of anonymity, of ordi-nariness was too painful for words.

It didn't help that esteem for motherhood was at an all-time low. I remember going to a party shortly after leaving work to be home with my baby and being asked what I did. I stammered something about staying home with a child and then felt demeaned and discounted as the person turned away, implying that therefore I had nothing interesting to say. I remember that moment as if it were yesterday. I can picture where I was standing. I can still recall the sense of unworthiness I struggled to keep at bay.

One could read this to mean that I think a "career" might have led more easily to self-actualization. Actually, as a young mother, I probably did feel that way, at least unconsciously, because it is easy to blame your unhappiness on an obvious factor, assuming that the alternative will magically solve the problem, much like a cow straining against the fence because the next field looks better.

Over time, I have come to realize that all women—indeed, all people—face these questions of purpose, values, and self-worth. If I speak through the voice of a struggling stay-at-home mom, I do not mean to imply superiority to any side of that issue: home, career, or otherwise. I speak from what I experienced, but I believe the issues are universal.

Other paths aren't easier; the questions just come at different times in different forms. The interrelationship of feminism/motherhood/work/social issues adds to the complexity. There is no magic bullet, no simple one-size-fits-all solution. Although grounded in the *Zeitgeist* of those late twentieth-century decades, my experiences were actually only the latest incarnation of age-old themes, themes that mothers and daughters have been struggling with since Biblical times.

What is success? That has been my relentless question as I've alternately bounded and foundered through adulthood. Those feelings of freedom and independence, that heady confidence I felt as a young single, came under repeated fire in the years that followed. *Womansong* reflects my experiences as I journeyed through the schizophrenic maze of choices women encounter as they go through their lives, trying to reconcile all the roles and possibilities open to or required of them. It has been a search for wholeness, for resolution, for compromise. How could I keep the best of the "old order" and also incorporate the long overdue rights of the new? How could I be myself, yet "fit in"? How could I reconcile ambition with motherhood and assertiveness with femininity? How did intelligence fit in? How could I have my own ideas but not be seen as pushy?

Life happens. The question is whether we want to live a "considered life" that is proactive or just take what comes and deal with it, which is reactive. For me, this has never been a question, because passivity doesn't seem to flow through my bones. The inkling of possibilities and opportunities goads me on to look, search, think, and consider. It whispers in my ear that balanced living is hard work, but it promises serendipity, satisfaction, and serenity.

This book is for women everywhere who struggle with these same questions. Maybe, like me, you will find strength in knowing that others share your quandaries. Perhaps my struggles can illuminate yours in the way that my friends, both real and literary, have done for me.

And so, the concert of metaphors begins. It beckons, challenging us to try out some new ways of looking at things.

It's never
too late
to be
who
you are

Subject

A melody…
which becomes a basic factor
in the structure of
the composition.

Love bears all things,
believes all things,
hopes all things,
endures all things.
LOVE NEVER FAILS.
I CORINTHIANS

The Splendors and Splinters of Love

Love is a many-splendored thing…
—PAUL F. WEBSTER

That's the familiar refrain, and anyone lucky enough to experience the heady, energizing, wondrous state of loving and being loved will wax poetic about love's many splendors.

Alas, love is also a many-splintered thing. Before love, we had only ourselves to consider and care for. When we love, other agendas encroach on our own. Not only do our lives become more meaningful and joyful, but they also become more complicated and demand difficult choices. These choices involve not only what is good for us personally, but also what is good for those we love, and those things are not always compatible. The many divergent needs and wishes of even the most loving couple or family render all sorts of plans, dreams, and good intentions into splinters. Yet, somehow, we persevere. Love's compensations and promise overshadow its drawbacks and beckon us onward.

It sounds so simple, this romantic concept that is love, as if the good and wonderful parts easily obliterate the limiting and difficult parts. Would that it was so, but the ineffable pleasures of love do not come without a price. We cannot have the joys of intimacy without its burdens. We cannot experience the delights of togetherness without also chafing at its constrictions now and then.

As a twenty-something, I became accustomed to going wherever I wanted, whenever I wanted. The only one to consult when deciding whether to buy something was my checkbook. I enjoyed the break from the complicated dynamics of living with my family and trying to please everyone. But—there is always a "but," isn't there? —I was also lonely and often daydreamed about sharing life with someone I loved.

Fast forward to married with children: I was no longer lonely; indeed, I was never alone. I could go nowhere without planning the logistics beforehand. Money decisions were exponentially more complicated. Now there were mouths to feed, house payments to make, and Responsibilities, capital R! Fast forward, again: teenagers needing attention, from the logistical to the philosophical. But what about me? Where did I fit in?

I am often accused of being a "Pollyanna," of having an insufferable and incurable silver-lining approach to life. "Get real," says a friend. "Admit that you're mad, you're unhappy, you're frustrated. Be like everybody else and acknowledge that you have moments of wanting to bag everything, go sit on an island with palm trees and soft ocean breezes and let someone else figure out how to deal with things."

Mea culpa. I certainly have felt anger, frustration, sadness, and anxiety, all these feelings hopelessly muddled and confused by guilt. Major guilt. You know the scenario: it's a variation on the how-can-you-not-eat-your-spinach-when-people-are-starving-in-Africa argument. It goes like this: here I am, a privileged, healthy, educated, white middle-class woman with a loving husband, wonderful children, a nice home, good friends, and ample food and warmth. How can I not be totally content with my life? How dare I ask, even in the stark, dark privacy of my own inner soul: Is this all there is? Why am I so selfish, not in actions—aha, a chink in the argument, since I never hesitate to do what needs to be done—but in ungrateful thoughts?

What is the source of this insidious dichotomy? Looking back, I think my inability to face negative thoughts is the dark side of having been taught to be so thoroughly positive and upbeat when I was a child. Perhaps it was a legacy from my parents' foothold in the Victorian era. My family, like many a fifties' family, danced around issues and maintained civility at almost any cost. Anger was frowned upon. Pouting, if silent, was tacitly allowed. Customary niceties like six o'clock family dinners took place on schedule with pasted-on smiles, regardless of how people were feeling or what domestic calamities had taken place. I didn't know how to deal with conflict because I grew up learning to avoid it. I was a sensitive child; unpleasantness and arguing (one person's discussion is another person's argument) left me feeling inordinately unsettled and threatened. My security, my sense of a safe haven in my surroundings, depended on my being able to make everyone happy. Can-do cheerfulness is certainly worth cultivating, but when it transforms from an attitude into a desperate necessity, it is unsustainable. No one can be all things to all people. No one, really, when all is said and done, can make anyone else "happy."

It's all so very complicated, especially since, as I look at families today, I see that many of them could use a good dose of simple civility. The crass, in-your-face, tell-it-all vulgarity pervasive in today's culture seems even more problematic than the false cheeriness that was the standard in my childhood household. Indefatigable cup-half-full optimism is probably the reason my mother lived to be ninety-eight; she was frail, wheelchair-bound, and in a nursing home—but cheerful. I am very, very thankful I was taught the importance of civility and respect for others. I just wish that honest communication skills had been part of the package.

At the time, it seemed that either you were polite or all hell would break loose; either you were well-mannered and courteous or you were headed for divorce court. I didn't know how to find middle ground, so my default behavior was avoidance of conflict. I was woefully unprepared for the inevitable frictions anyone would feel when experiencing the mixed blessings of a wonderful relationship that also rearranges and alters your personal parameters.

My first breakthrough was to name this problem. It took me a good long time to be able to admit that even something as wondrous as love has its thorns, demanding cautious handling or removal. We do not solve what we cannot name, and we do not name what we are afraid to face. If we can put aside fear and listen to our inner truths, we can name our demons and begin to find ways to tame them. If we dare to seek truth, we will be liberated from illusory limitations. We will be free in ways we've never been free in the time before we risked being totally honest with ourselves.

In time, I have come to see love's splinters as blessings in disguise. The same thorns that might seem to be tearing two people apart alternately can be used as building blocks on the road to wholeness, if only we can figure out how to listen to them, work with them, and incorporate their messages into some sort of personal cohesion. We must not allow niggling, negative thoughts to threaten us. We need to drag them out in the open, let the light of day shine on them, and figure out how to reframe them and work with them instead of denying them!

Are you beset with feelings of lost privacy, of wishing you had your own space, a "room of your own" in which to be messy, to create, to read, to cry, to do whatever you please without being asked what you are doing? If so, you need to say so, if only in the privacy of your own mind. It is important to look such thoughts straight in the eye, admit them, and then ask yourself how you can compensate or compromise or find alternatives that address your concerns. We stunt our ability to grow and to cope when we try to pretend our concerns are not frustrating and daunting. You aren't a bad person because you have downbeat thoughts or because you see the problems and challenges as well as the blessings; you're human.

What eluded me was the realization that I did not need to be perfect. After all, wholeness means all the parts, not just the good parts. Chafing at restrictions in a relationship does not mean that you love someone any less. In the timeless words of Shakespeare, "Love is not love which alters when it alteration finds." Love simply is. It does not ask, nor does it require. It bears all things, including a little show of temper now and then. Love leads to endless possibilities if you can surrender to it humbly, knowing that your best effort will be "good enough."

Splendors and splinters: you can't have one without the other. Together they form the melody underlying everything you think, feel, and do. Indeed, splendors and splinters are the "subject," the most basic factors in the composition that is your life. Any attempt to achieve balance must begin with acceptance and appreciation of this paradoxical dichotomy.

> *Love, the supreme musician,*
> *is always playing in our souls.*
>
> —RUMI

make friends
with freedom
and uncertainty

SARK

Cantus Firmus

*A pre-existent melody which
is made the basis of a polyphonic
composition by the addition of
contrapuntal voices.*

when your heart speaks,
take good notes.

JUDITH CAMPBELL

Voiceprint

Deep inside,
my own unique
"signature song" awaits,
begging to be sung.

Never mind what the *Harvard Dictionary of Music* says; to me *cantus firmus* has always meant strong *(firmus)* melody *(cantus).* A strong melody might almost by definition be pre-existent, as if it had always been there. Surely, that is the sense that music historians portray. Melodies are as old as humankind. They surfaced in the record in medieval times and were gradually enhanced and elaborated upon and made into more complex forms.

The description of a pre-existent melody provides an apt metaphor for considering who you are, who you truly are. I believe a strong melody exists that is "my own song," my *cantus firmus,* a melody within me as old as time and creation, one that has always been there, waiting to emerge and be enhanced. Alas, there are also many other strong melodies wafting through the atmosphere, almost teasing me. Perhaps that faint one, there: maybe that's my own song. No, wait: listen to that other one; maybe that's it…and on it goes.

Searching for genuine integrity, your own true voice, leads us to two major possibilities: one is passive; the alternate is active and deliberately engaged.

One could say that the passive route is the default setting that unconsciously lures us to buy into current cultural expectations. In the passive scenario, we soak up and imitate popular culture. This process can be insidiously subtle as it gathers bits and pieces of expectations from television shows, magazine and newspaper articles, movie characters, how the relatives live, advertising hype, public opinion, and so forth. It is insidious and subtle in that we think all the while that we have "chosen" these opinions and ways to live. It is insidious and subtle because often we do not even realize we're being sold a bill of goods and are living a set of behaviors without even considering what they mean, without considering whether they are consistent with our core values.

Most of us wander in and out of this mode, whether we intend to or not. We like to believe that we think for ourselves, but none of us truly does that with any consistency, because we do not exist in a vacuum. There are always influences, trends, and people we hope to impress; there are always circumstances that tint the glasses through which we are looking at things.

I think back to the early seventies, when my new husband and I decided to buy land, build a house, be self-reliant, and get "back to the land." These were good moves based on good motives, but they were hardly autonomous: we were enormously influenced by the counter-culture upheaval of the Hippie Sixties.

I look in my closet and realize how many, many times over the years I have tried to find my "fashion personality." Ha! We wear some variation of what the Seventh Avenue fashion industry decrees we will wear. That's not wrong, but if I think I'm making up my own mind about how to dress, I'm kidding myself. Making up my own mind is, in the best, practical sense, some compromise between what is "out there" and what is inside my heart and mind. Cultural traditions and shared ideas are the glue of a society. We need that glue. Yet mindless compliance is unhealthy; it prevents natural checks and balances that would keep inane ideas and trends from growing out of proportion and poisoning the cultural milieu. Daring to be different creates diversity; always being different just for the sake of being different, risks anarchy. The reality check that is our means of gauging personal authenticity is being able to recognize the motivation behind a specific choice.

The status quo carries with it incredible forces for perpetuating itself.

If we can train ourselves to be aware that popular culture and societal expectations are trying to draw us into the prevailing cultural imperatives, we can learn to weigh what we observe and decide if it is personally appropriate and relevant.

Move to the country? Fine, if country living appeals to you. Wear capri pants? Why not, if they are comfortable and fit the self-image you're comfortable maintaining. Just don't confuse those choices with your inborn *cantus firmus,* that "magical music deep inside" that is your real, genuine, authentic essence. Country life and capris are only outward manifestations. While they represent value judgments and choices, they are not the ultimate expressions that define who you are.

The other possibility, then, is to renounce the default setting and embrace the adventure. Search for those harmonics that resonate with the "real person" inside by deliberately considering your circumstances and alternatives. It is hard work to take this considered path. It takes thoughtfulness, vigilance, persistence, energy, commitment, honesty, guts, and faith. Most of all, it takes intention, the intention to decide once again on each new day to seek, to think, to listen, to be open to possibility, and to willingly stumble, pick yourself up, and start again.

So, is the answer within or without? The journey starts with two ideas, two contrasting possibilities.

Sing songs that none have sung.

—PARAMAHANSA YOGANANDA

The Judging Witness

Life is an endless recruiting of witnesses.
—CAROL SHIELDS, *THE STONE DIARIES*

In 1997, I happened upon a book by Dalma Heyn called *Marriage Shock: The Transformation of Women into Wives*. It continues to amaze me that this little book went largely unrecognized and undiscussed. The only commentary I subsequently came across implied that this was a selfish, one-sided, feminist view of marriage. I took something very different from Heyn's book: I saw it as definitively pro-marriage. It advocates that marriage "be moved from the realm of power into the realm of pleasure, where mutuality and reciprocity replace hierarchy and control." Heyn makes her case through a fascinating review of the sociological and cultural foundations of marriage, showing how it has evolved because of economic expediencies. Take, for example, the agrarian focus of the seventeen hundreds, which was followed by the Industrial Revolution in the eighteen hundreds.

Heyn coins the term "the Witness" to describe an amorphous voice that pressures women to transmogrify when they marry into an iconographic image of the Ideal Wife. Doing so is to take the passive route of accepting cultural imperatives. The point is, no one tells women to do this, to become "an anachronistic, unreal model of womanhood that has materialized along with her wedding ring, has moved into her home uninvited. This is a tireless icon who is relaxed, sexually eager but not too, attractive yet modest, nurturing and giving and caring, like the memory of some long-lost angel." This message is a non-genetic cultural transmission, an example of what evolutionary biologist Richard Dawkins calls a meme, a unit "that conveys the idea of cultural transmission, or unit of imitation... Memes are to our minds what genes are to our bodies, ideas that have the power to determine the way we think in the same way that genes have the power to determine, say, the way we look."

All this sounds very scholarly and theoretical, but Heyn is onto something here, something important that many of us have neglected to realize. The Judging Witness looms in the background of our minds like some Invincible Authority. It lectures us, admonishes us, and makes us feel small, unworthy, and dependent. It short-circuits relationality. A relationship involves give and take, negotiation, discussion, and interaction. When the Judging Witness is in residence, we are on a one-way street. It obstructs interaction by shutting it off before there is any exchange between wife and husband. This isn't about women's rights, feminist power, or who gets whose way, or any other "socially radical" construct. Everyone loses when honest communication is thwarted. Instead of trust and mutuality, an air of calculated posturing pervades the atmosphere. Role-playing replaces authenticity.

Finally, we have a name for the source of those irrational "shoulds" that somehow get incorporated into our psyches. Aha! Nowhere is it written that a "good wife" is supposed to become some new, different person when she leaves the marriage ceremony. Nowhere does it say that she should defer to a husband in any different way than she would defer to anyone she might live with or care about. There is nothing radical about disagreeing with a husband! But the examples we've lived with—in my case, my mother's total deference to my father—become irrational witnesses, implying rules where, actually, only tacit agreements exist, or existed.

This conceptualization allows us to understand the source of our conflicting ideas about what it means to be a wife. "Light-bulb moments" seem so self-evident in retrospect, yet they are heavily veiled and unreachable until someone presents those thoughts directly. We must recognize the Judging Witness in order to dispel it. Those supposed requirements we imagine, those roles we think we need to fulfill, some—if not many, if not most—are actually just culturally imposed messages that only we can evaluate and adopt or dispel for ourselves.

> *We have to see, I think,*
> *that questioning the values of old rules is*
> *different from simply breaking them.*
>
> —ELIZABETH JANEWAY

The Genuine Witness

The alternative to unexamined, wholesale adoption of the cultural/societal and amorphous forms of the Judging Witness is beautifully described in the following piece written by Alan Cohen. Women lovingly copy and distribute it among their friends, making it a sort of talisman for the journey of self-discovery.

They're Singing Your Song

When a woman in a certain African tribe knows she is pregnant, she goes out into the wilderness with a few friends and together they pray and meditate until they hear the song of a child. They recognize that every soul has its own vibration that expresses its unique flavor and purpose. When the women attune to the song, they sing it out loud. Then they return to the tribe and teach it to everyone else.

When the child is born, the community gathers and sings the child's song to him or her. Later, when the child enters education, the village gathers and chants the child's song. When the child passes through the initiation into adulthood, the people again come together and sing. At the time of marriage, the person hears his or her own song.

In the African tribe, there is one other occasion upon which the villagers sing to the child. If at any time during his or her life, the person commits a crime or aberrant social act, the individual is called to the center of the village and the people in the community form a circle around them. Then they sing their song to them.

The tribe recognizes that the correction for antisocial behavior is not punishment; it is love and the remembrance of identity. When you recognize your own song, you have no desire or need to do anything that would hurt another.

A friend is someone who knows your song and sings it to you when you have forgotten it. Those who love you are not fooled by mistakes you have made or dark images you hold about yourself. They remember your beauty when you feel ugly; your wholeness when you are broken; your innocence when you feel guilty; and your purpose when you are confused.

You may not have grown up in an African tribe that sings your song to you at crucial life transitions, but life is always reminding you when you are in tune with yourself and when you are not. When you feel good, what you are doing matches your song, when you feel awful, it doesn't. In the end, we shall all recognize our song and sing it well. You may feel a little warbly at the moment, but so have all great singers. Just keep singing and you'll find your way home.

—BY ALAN COHEN

From *They're Playing Your Song*

Sprout Where You Are Planted

*...the growth of understanding
follows an ascending spiral rather
than a straight line.*

—JOANNA FIELD

Cantus firmus, our pre-existent melody, is a complex thing. It is informative to look at the within/without polarities and possibilities, but these do not exist independently of each other. How can we begin to take these melodic threads and weave them into the coherent compositions—our lives—that surely are possible if we are truly reaching for the stars, for the very best selves we were destined to be? How can we grasp this apogee of possibility?

Synthesis is possible. Not easy, not quick, but possible. Gradually, we can come to feel entitled to dreams and aspirations that have nothing to do with husbands, children, or surface societal expectations. Resolutions begin with a surrender of sorts, when we first dare to listen for our *cantus firmus,* that true inner voice. That first leap of daring to look at things differently is the hardest step. Then, taking baby steps from there, we need to embrace that voice, believe in it, and finally, start to explore where it is leading.

Personally, I had been stuffing my private longings into an imaginary box, cramming it shut, and fiercely holding down the lid, secretly afraid that if I looked at independent dreams I'd be seduced into abandoning my family. Somewhere was a voice whispering, "All or nothing," when, in reality, what was called for was a combination of knowing my own heart and doing creative problem solving.

As I dared to really, really think about those "forbidden" ideas, I came up with some surprises: I didn't really want the full-time, totally engrossing job that I suspected would sideline so many of the family activities that were precious, not only to me, but also to my family: trips to the library; cooking together; time for long, impromptu discussions with my growing children; as well as the freedom to "be there" for them. I liked, really liked, much of my independent existence as a wife, mother, and homemaker. What I needed was something outside and beyond those responsibilities, something that was my personal endeavor, something that used my unique talents and passions. I needed to define myself as something other than my husband's wife or my children's mother, not to the exclusion of those roles, but in harmonious combination with them.

The challenge was to allow my inner voice to come forth, be heard, and blossom. Only then could I begin to find a creative way to channel it within the parameters necessary to ensure the quality of our life as a family. I didn't have the answer, but at least I'd defined the question.

Dwell in possibility

Interlude

Any type of inserted music.

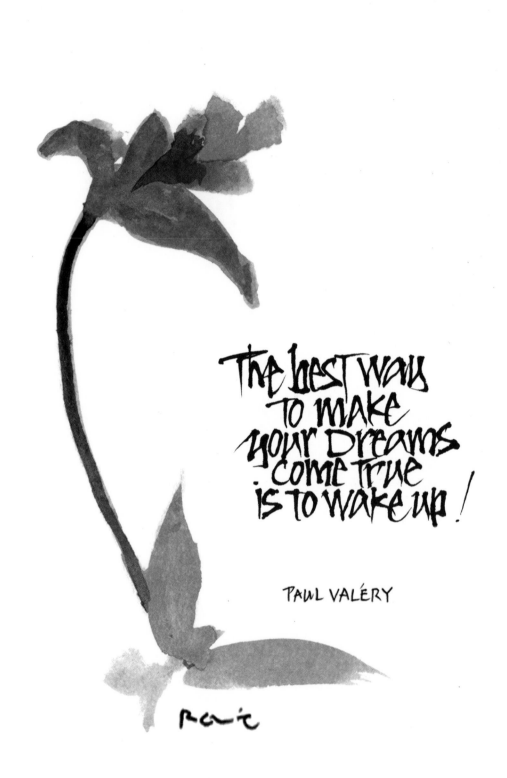

The best way
to make
your Dreams
come true
is to wake up!

PAUL VALÉRY

Living the Questions— Now

Be patient and kind toward all that is unresolved
in your heart
And try to love the questions themselves.
Do not seek answers that cannot be given you
Because you would not be able to live them.
And the point is to live everything.
Live the questions now.
Perhaps you will gradually, without noticing it,
Live some distant day into the answers.

—RAINER MARIA RILKE

Live the questions now. Rilke's advice is strangely comforting. It gently chides us to stop wanting pat, tidy answers and to realize that the questions are in themselves valuable. It can be difficult to be gracious about this when we are mired eyeball-deep in questions and uncertainty. However, questions are the doors to new places and new thoughts, to growth, and to opportunities. Indeed, we must learn to love them. Perhaps that sounds like banal cheerleading, but it is a message we need to remember again, again, and yet again.

The central quest of my adult life has been searching for a definition of work that I could both believe in and live with. Just what is "work," anyway? Although I felt starkly alone with my question, I was merely one of untold scores of women who have left traditional workplace jobs to stay home and raise children. The change of venue changes and challenges our sense of where we fit in the scheme of things. Like a low-grade fever, this aching question of where we fit in nags at us and drags us down. There are so many demands on us. We are so tired, so splintered, and have so many important things to do at once. And then, as we struggle with this question, along comes some well-meaning soul who inquires, "Do you work?" Somehow the implied definition of "work" never seems to include the necessities of homemaking, housekeeping, and childcare. "Work" to most of us means "jobs done for money in the public sphere." Gender expectations about work linger, also, in spite of Herculean efforts to expand the breadth of possibilities for both women and men.

The reality of the present cultural milieu in our society is that it places little value on the art of motherhood and raising children. We are surrounded with evidence of the folly of this point of view, yet it persists. Nonetheless, I knew that, for me, nothing could be more important than giving my children the good, solid, stable start in life that is achieved by staying at home with them in their early years. The clash between the demeaning social ethos that discounts the efforts of stay-at-home moms and my intuitive conviction, which impelled me to go against that ethos, was gut wrenching. The media are still awash with messages such as "quality time, not quantity time," implying that caregiving is a sort of extracurricular activity to be "handled" after "work." In such a toxic climate, incessant, noisy questions festered in my soul like static on a poorly tuned radio: Shouldn't I go back to "work"? Am I worth anything if I "just" stay home? Why can't I do everything, be a Supermom?

In order to get rid of the static and tune in more clearly, I needed another way to look at this issue. When you aren't finding answers to your questions, perhaps you are asking the wrong questions. There are always answers—always! —if you ask the right questions. No solutions or answers were forthcoming to my questions about work. None. I was at a stalemate. I was absolutely, completely stuck; deadlocked, with no illumination, no resolution, no clues—nothing. At such times, it is essential to ask: How else can I look at this? How can I ask a different question?

Sometimes the "different question" does not come in the form of a query, but in the attitude of being open to receiving an idea. We can let a thought, a reading, a speech, a movie, or a work of art speak for the questions we don't know to ask. During my working-identity stalemate, I heard by chance a television interview in which the guest observed that it has become the custom in our society to define people by what they "do," rather than by what they "are." Tongue in cheek, the guest went on to suggest that when someone asks you what you do, you should reply, "About what?"

Hearing that exchange, the question I hadn't been able to dredge from my depths exploded: Do I believe that what matters about people is whether they check groceries, teach music, or perform heart surgery? Or do I believe that what matters is what they stand for, what they believe in, and whether they are responsible, contributing citizens? We all are to blame for this identity confusion, myself included. We have internalized that conversation-opener, "So what do you do?" It would be far more appropriate to ask people what they care about or what they are interested in. Such questions would not only validate a far broader range of choices, all of which are important to the health of society, they also would give recognition to underlying values that are the very groundwork of civilization: respect, tolerance, community, and diversity, to name a few.

The idea of knowing people by their interests and values instead of by their job titles did not come in time to help me when I was in the trenches with kids, dishes, Cub Scouts, and music lessons. What did help was a cooperative effort with my husband to consider how we were dividing responsibility for our family's requirements. We figured out that there was no way each of us could do everything. It's comical, really, that something so obvious would take "figuring out." As we looked around at people we knew, we observed that all couples make their own deals, often without even realizing that is what they are doing. Couples have unspoken agreements that typically evolve slowly, without examination or discussion. That's fine when things are working to mutual satisfaction, but often one party or the other will begin to outgrow this tacit agreement and find him/herself tongue-tied, stuck in a mode without really knowing why. Getting "unstuck" requires—you guessed it—braving the questions once again.

My early family years were fun, frustrating, poignant, and full of learning, growing, laughing, and crying—a microcosm of all life's possibilities. Feeling useful is never in question when you are surrounded by the patter of little feet. I knew what I was doing was important; I was rewarded constantly by my children's devotion and progress. And yet, there was a sense of worthlessness that I never could quite dispel completely because the prevailing voice of the era was touting the myth of "doing it all." And there I was, doing just a portion of "it," and the unsung portion, no less.

My husband and I had long discussions about what our needs were and who could best do what. In our case, when it came time to consider the early stages of parenthood, the traditional pattern emerged: my husband had greater earning power, and I had real interest in home, hearth, and child rearing. I knew I wanted to be home with my babies. Fortunately, my husband valued my contribution. He often told me that our family's quality of life depended on the things I did. I couldn't see beyond the pre-school years. I had no idea what I'd want or be able to do when my children reached school age, but that was a problem for another day.

When both my children were finally in school, "another day" came. Then the question became a strong, constant presence in my mind, noisily chattering about moving on. Alas, on to what? I discovered to my horror that I was terrified of re-entering the work world. I had a Master's degree from one of the world's leading universities, yet I wasn't sure I could handle anything of value in the nine-to-five world. This is perhaps the single, most insidious by-product experienced by modern, stay-at-home moms: after a while, they themselves start believing that they have nothing of value to contribute to society as a whole. I did everything I could to deny these thoughts. I procrastinated. I made myself artificially busy. I read escapist novels, one after another.

One morning, I realized with sudden clarity that I had read one novel too many. The plots all seemed the same, and I realized I was reading about life instead of living it. The questions resurfaced, refusing to be denied or ignored. The time had come to face these scary thoughts and get on with life.

This was the conundrum: I had time for some pursuit beyond home and childcare, but not enough time for a typical, full-time job, if, as a family, we wanted to sustain the lifestyle that we had so carefully created.

I needed some as-yet-undefined project or job of my own, something that did not involve either my husband or my children. I spent months stuck at this point, trying to think what I could do. It was pretty discouraging. The nation's workplaces were not then family-friendly, nor are they now, on the whole.

One fateful day, my husband said, "Why don't you just go to an employment agency?" I was tempted to shut him off by telling him all the reasons that wouldn't solve anything, but I decided I should have an open mind. It would be an enlightening experience to see if my pessimism was warranted. Perhaps there was something "out there" that I had missed.

Unfortunately, my perceptions were accurate. I was told very politely that there were lots of openings I qualified for if I was willing to work full-time. I remember reporting back to my husband.

"Well?" he asked. "What did they say?"

"Do you want the good news or the bad news?" I asked.

"The good."

"Well, there is no good news, because unless I want to work full-time, the agency has absolutely no suggestions about how I might find an appropriate position."

Something good did happen that day, however. Finally, instead of feeling downtrodden and unworthy, I got mad. Suddenly, I was ready to realize that I wasn't the problem. There wasn't anything wrong with me. The problem was the way society and the workplace had concurrently developed to a point where families were hard put to find workable solutions. Once I stopped feeling defensive, it was much easier to wrestle with the issues and figure out what to do about them. Once again, the tool that turned an amorphous issue into something I could get my hands on was the act of questioning.

I reframed my thoughts into questions: What were my givens? Where did I have flexibility? How much money did I need to make? Did I have abilities and talents that I was overlooking? How much time did I really need to take care of my family the way I wanted the job done?

As I thought about family, work, social structures, time, and activities, I concluded that quality family life leaves room for about one and a half "typical" full-time jobs per household. Two people working forty-five to fifty or more hours per week (I know of no professionals who manage to work "just" forty hours) simply do not have sufficient time for all the other things family living should include, like sit-down-together meals where real conversation can take place and time to help children with homework, listen to heartaches when they happen, play games, send Aunt Ilse a birthday card, or take the dog to the vet. There simply is not enough flexibility in two overly-full agendas to work in these things, unless parents get far too little sleep, have far too little time to breathe, and have very little time for themselves or each other.

The lucky, energizing truth of my situation was that I had options. I had lots of options. I had been focusing on the problems instead of on the possibilities. Working full-time was out of the question, but I was ignoring the fact that I didn't need "full-time" income. I couldn't see where I would fit in, but that didn't mean that a position fitting my needs did not exist. It just meant that, to find it, I had to look harder and be more creative. I needed to stop blaming existing circumstances and go make new ones!

Spending time with career exploration materials, I took a fresh look at my skills, talents, values, and desires. I found that I needed to ask not One Big Question, What do I want to be?, but many small questions, such as, How much time do I have? Do I want to work with people, things, or ideas? What am I interested in? What are my workplace values?

The answers to the "little" questions converged to reveal multiple career possibilities, all of which fit my wants and needs profile. I had thought I was looking for the One Perfect Thing That Is My Destiny. Instead, I discovered that there were actually many intriguing possibilities, any of which could be rewarding and fulfilling and provide the individual, creative outlet that was missing from my life. I needed great flexibility to preserve the family routines we treasured, but I didn't need a lot of money. I decided to look for positions where I could negotiate for time instead of money.

Once this concept crystallized, my life was transformed. A career counselor supplied the final dose of ammunition I needed to have the courage to knock on doors: "Remember that looking for the ideal job is a lot like looking for a needle in a haystack. You don't find it on the first try. But every time someone says no, you're statistically one step closer to the yes you're looking for." In other words, being turned down is not necessarily personal, which is something the re-entering housewife often has difficulty remembering. Just keep looking, keep talking, and keep asking until you turn the laws of probability in your favor.

As it happened, because I had focused on realistic possibilities, I got the first job I asked for. I had read about a college-planning service in a local newspaper. It sounded interesting and rewarding, and it seemed like a good fit. It required the job skills I had identified as ones I wanted to utilize. I summoned a newfound sense of chutzpah and dialed the number. After all, I realized, if I didn't get the job, I wouldn't be any worse off than before. I asked to speak to the president and talked my way into an appointment for an interview. The interview gave me an opportunity to express openness and willingness to learn. A revelation occurred: I got hired because I had the nerve to risk asking to be hired!

Good questioning is linked also to patience. Oh, I know, who wants to be patient when action is required, and required now? But is it required now? Or do we just imagine that there is no time to wait for illumination? If I am trying to decide whether to drive to Boston to see my daughter when there may be some snow en route, obviously there comes a time when I must decide either to go or to stay home. If, however, I am trying to discern my next career move or how to deal with someone I find difficult, I need to cultivate patience and ask as many questions as I can possibly put together. I should expect to experience an incubation period in which ideas can gel and solutions can become evident, while remaining open-minded so that I can recognize an answer when it comes to light.

And so I ask again: Just what is "work," anyway? *The American Heritage Dictionary* defines it as "physical or mental effort or activity directed toward the production or accomplishment of something." It doesn't say anything about monetary compensation. Work means accomplishing something. Period. I suspect the happiest work is accomplishing something for which we have enthusiasm, and indeed, even that is by no means static. No doubt our enthusiasms will change and point to different "work" at different stages of our lives.

Questioning is not a tidy process. It is hard to plan for it. If your intuition whispers that the evolving line of inquiry may lead to a "forbidden" or uncomfortable place, you may be reluctant to embrace the uncertainty or disinclined to create uneasy tremors in the status quo. What if my thoughts about returning to work shake up household routines and create resentments and pandemonium? What if my husband and kids don't want to rearrange their schedules just because I may want to rearrange mine? What if communication falls apart and Pandora's box springs open, never to close again? Once you start asking questions, it seems that more and more of them pop to the surface, some of them useful and others paralyzing. Nonetheless, despite all the accompanying negative possibilities, we must refuse to let fear, ambivalence, and uncertainty derail a robust and faithful commitment to questioning. Questions are forerunners to solutions. No questions: no contemplation. No contemplation: no growth. No growth: ultimately, no life.

Buddhist teachings, as I understand them, contribute another dimension to the relationship between questioning and personal growth. The Buddhist way is readiness of mind. Elegantly simple, Buddhist writings suggest that awareness of the oneness of all things is the basis of wisdom. We are not separate beings; we only think we are. We grow when we learn to accept what "is" without judgment, which includes accepting questions and unknowns. Even when we cannot fathom answers, the Buddhist way reminds us that our questions are merely part of a greater whole that is not yet within our grasp. Rilke's words point out that we cannot understand what we are not ready to understand. When we surrender to these things, we open ourselves to "living some distant day into the answers." The answers are there; we just don't know them, yet. As we learn to live with questions, to listen to them, and to work with them, the answers will come forth in their own time. Mindfulness is the path to their discovery.

Being happy in our endeavors requires diligent attention to the small voices inside us, the voices quietly but persistently singing. *Cantus firmus,* our inborn songs, beckon us toward growth, change, and discovery. Our challenge is to be brave enough to refuse to be pigeonholed into the same small definition for all of our days. Our challenge is to let each stage's solutions shine in full glory until their usefulness has passed, and then to segue as gracefully as possible into the next adventure. Questions, the inner mind's way of speaking to the conscious self, provide the way to growth and change.

Open-mindedness—the ability to look, listen, consider, and strive for new combinations of thoughts and possibilities—is the single most powerful means of unleashing the maximum potential that lies within each of us, waiting to germinate, sprout, and grow. Questioning is the vehicle of open-mindedness. Back to Square One: we must learn to love the questions.

Take time to work.
It is the price of success.
Take time to meditate.
It is the source of power.
Take time to play.
It is the secret of perpetual youth.
Take time to read.
It is the way to knowledge.
Take time to be friendly.
It is the road to
        happiness.
Take time to laugh.
It is the music of the soul.
And take time to love
and be loved.

OLD IRISH PRAYER

Counterpoint

Note against note, voice against voice.
Combination into single musical fabric of lines
which have distinctive melodic significance,
two [or more] points of view.

The next
message
you need
is
right
where
you are.

RAM DASS

FIRST
MOVEMENT:
Two Variations on a Theme

The Ultimately Undeniable Inner Voice: Do? Be? Do? BE!

"Dooby Dooby Doo..."

—IKE TURNER

To be or to do: that is the question. Whether 'tis nobler in the mind to suffer the slings and arrows of endless doings, or to take the quieter, inner road of concentrating on being. (My apologies to Shakespeare.) This is perhaps the ultimate question: Are you what you do or what you are? Which are more important: your accomplishments or your values/beliefs/thoughts?

When I was young, the do side easily won out. The seduction of recognition, of wanting to "be somebody" was irresistible. This is not to say that I was willing to sell out on my values; not at all. However, when values and accomplishments were at odds, I felt a certain sense of loss when sticking to those values required sacrificing some potential accomplishment. I had trouble believing that what I stood for, my being, was enough justification for the space I take up on this earth. It was hard to distinguish the components: ego, values, necessities, essence—I could go on and on with this line of thought and get increasingly amorphous and metaphysical, which is exactly the problem. This do-be business is evanescent; it calls like a siren in the fog.

As a "doer," I worked doggedly at any tangible project I undertook.

Teaching wasn't an eight-to-four, five-day-a-week job; it was all consuming. How else would I be good enough? If I wasn't in the classroom, I was planning lessons and rehearsals. If I wasn't planning, I was researching new music or counseling lonely students. Fast-forward to motherhood, and again the picture is full of doing. I was constantly busy with not only the necessary care-type things, but also with reading about how to do them best, forming playgroups, volunteering in the community, and learning to garden, sew, and preserve bounty. How else would I be worth anything?

Later, when my children were older and I had more flexibility, I was consumed with what I could do to make money. That's not necessarily a bad thing, but I wanted to do it for the wrong reason: I wanted the respect that our society seems to give only to those who "make" money. Ah, yes: wanting respect isn't a bad thing, either, but obsessing about making money to get respect reveals that I had been indoctrinated most effectively (if unintentionally) into our society's predilection to value everything in dollars and cents.

Beyond my obsession with paid work, another drumbeat echoed softly yet insistently in the back of my mind: all this emphasis on accomplishments, remunerated or not, is for naught unless I am living my values. St. Paul's words called to me across the ages: "I may speak in tongues of men and angels, but if I am without love, I am a sounding gong or a clanging cymbal." Herein lies an intimation of resolution between the forces of doing and being.

Love is first. Plain and simple. Doing is important, but only if you are doing what you love. And to do what you love, you first must be who you are, not someone else's vision of who you are or who they think you ought to be. Harvey Fierstein, the actor, playwright, and screenwriter, says it succinctly and powerfully, "Accept no one's definition of your life. Define yourself." No one else is as good at being me as I am. If I combine this concept with my belief that I was created for a purpose, then I can stop trying so hard to fit into a given mold and instead be on the lookout for places where I fit naturally, no cramming required!

Treya Killam Wilber wrestles honestly and articulately with the do/be dilemma in *Grace and Grit*, the book she wrote with her husband about cancer, spirituality, life, healing, and death. She talks about throwing over many feminine values, "A denial, I believe, of my feminine side, my body, my nurturing, my sexuality, while I aligned myself with my head, my father, my logic, my society's values…I need to learn how to read the depths of my being, find my own 'guidance'…"

When Ken Wilber, Treya's husband, comments on her do/be deliberations, he confirms this insight about the importance of owning one's inner qualities, that unique combination of genes, memes, experiences, and ideas that make me the best me there is. Wilber, understanding that Treya has equated floundering for purpose with innate worthlessness, writes: "You think that because you haven't found your ultimate vocation…you are worthless. You'll find it, I'm sure. But in the meantime, you completely overlook your being, your presence, your energy, your integrity…We all love you for what you are, not what you do," he tells her. He goes on to define being versus doing. "Being meant: letting go and letting God, accepting, trusting, faith, forgiving. Doing meant: assuming responsibility for those things, and only those things, that can be changed, and then working as hard as you can toward changing them."

In the musical form counterpoint, two melodic phrases are needed to form the backbone of a fugue. Similarly, it takes both the "doing" and the "being" to fully define our essence, which is the inner core of our being that makes each one of us who we are. To ignore or bypass either factor, to favor one over the other, is like listening to only one part or voice of a musical composition that was written for several parts. It doesn't make much sense without all the parts. Like an echo, you get a sense, a glimmer, of the parts, but not the full, rich resonance of the whole, enriched by the nuance of interplay.

Slowly the conundrum unravels: You must live up to real responsibilities, being careful not to manufacture ones that are not real. For example, learning about gardening is not part of a mother's job description. Beyond "real" responsibilities, what you love should be allowed to lead you where it will. Those real responsibilities are enough. Once they are taken care of, daydreaming on a summer day is totally "worthy." So are playing the piano, reading, thinking, playing with children, cooking, dawdling, trying a new art form, or taking a chance on, say, writing a book. What's important, beyond being a basic good citizen of the world, is to "follow your bliss." After all, it was God who gave you your bliss, and God wants you to use it!

Nothing can bring you peace but yourself.

—RALPH WALDO EMERSON

The Dorothea Imbroglio

...and Dorothea: she had no dreams of
being praised above other women...Her full nature
spent itself in deeds which have no great name on the earth,
but the effect of her being on those around her was
incalculable, for the growing good of the world is partly
dependent on unhistoric acts, and all those Dorotheas
who live faithfully their hidden lives, and rest
in invisible tombs.

—GEORGE ELIOT, *MIDDLEMARCH*

I didn't read this quote; I heard it first on a PBS production. It struck me like lightning. Thankfully, I had recorded the production and could go back, replay it, and copy down these words. They fleshed out the quandary I'd been feeling about anonymity. I came to call this problem "Dorothea" in my mind, and I played with words in an attempt to classify how I felt about it. Was it a syndrome? My dictionary says a syndrome indicates disease or an abnormal condition, so that was not it. Dorotheas are anonymous, not sick or weird. Was it a condition, which is defined as "a state of being," which also has negative possibilities? I looked up quandary in the thesaurus and found "predicament," "circumstance," and "imbroglio." Imbroglio! That's what it is: "a difficult or intricate situation, an entanglement." The "Dorothea Imbroglio." Like chameleons, Dorotheas tirelessly adapt to changing needs, often constraining their own dreams and ambitions. They are entangled in the ordinary and must either learn to be content with that or figure out how to incorporate something extraordinary in their lives.

We Dorotheas are women who grapple with impossible demands and try to find ways to combine career and family roles and reconcile societal expectations with our dreams of self-fulfillment. We ricochet among tasks, often mired in the mundane but longing for just a touch of the profound. We do it for respect, for some sense that we are important in the larger scheme of things. We struggle to make creative choices. We compromise. We swim upstream, pleading for part-time work or jobs that fit our needs and learning to run our own businesses so we can play by rules that work for real families. Our lives are tapestries of many threads: our jobs, our husbands, our children, our families, our talents, our interests, our homes, our friends, and the community organizations we support.

A tapestry is an apt metaphor. The single threads that make up tapestries, taken one by one, are usually unremarkable. Their beauty and significance emerge when they are combined. Furthermore, a tapestry cannot exist without knots to tie the piece together. Threads (beauty) and knots (necessity): the whole of a tapestry or of a life cannot exist without both the beautiful threads and the utilitarian knots. You don't argue with the knots in a tapestry; when you're out of thread, you tie a knot and go on. So it is, too, with life. When you get tied up with necessities, think of them as knots that tie together a larger pattern. It takes rows upon rows of threads to reveal the picture in a tapestry. It takes years upon years to reveal the significance and meaning of your daily trials and triumphs.

It can be hard to hold on to that long view in the midst of multiple responsibilities, those common, everyday, unheralded, unfashionable, only-noticed-if-they're-undone tasks. They can wear you down and unravel your fragile perspective and the delicate truce you've struck with yourself to justify your choices within your circumstances, especially when ego shows up at the scene.

Personally, my "baggage" has always been wound up in questions about ego. I have found it difficult, at times, to decide how to draw the line between a healthy sense of self-esteem and conceit, or arrogance, both in myself and in my perceptions of other people. I can see why I struggle: ego is defined both as "an appropriate pride in oneself, that is, self-esteem," and "an exaggerated sense of self-importance; conceit." The former is my goal, the latter the specter that inhibits me. The challenge is to achieve balance, to cultivate enough self-esteem without bringing on conceit.

We need to feel good about our skills and abilities, but not so good that we suffer the delusion that we're generally superior to others. That's the rub: we need to learn to feel specifically confident—where appropriate—without falling into the trap of generalizing our greatness to categories where it is not present. I happen to have perfect pitch. In this rather rare musical ability, I am "superior" to most other people. This does not, however, carry over to any other quality. Nor is superiority—imagined or real—necessarily significant! We are what we are.

The journey to self-knowledge is extremely personal and individual, as varied as are people themselves. For me, the key to unlocking confidence in my personal skills and abilities was learning about personality types through the Myers-Briggs Type Indicator®. (The Myers-Briggs Type Indicator® is a personality inventory based on the theories of psychologist Carl Jung.)

Type knowledge gives us the means to understand why we react to things in the ways we do. It provides a useful lens for viewing human behavior, which is particularly important if you happen to be surrounded by people of other types, as I have been. There are reasons for why we are the way we are. Understanding those reasons enables us to be more effective in our social interactions.

Learning to recognize my personal strengths was a liberating affirmation. Finally, I could stop beating myself up for what I'm not and concentrate on making the most of what I am. I may have a hard time with criticism, but the flip side is that I am naturally empathetic. Just knowing my tendency to feel criticized already begins to remove the sting and help me to learn to be more objective. Conversely, I know that my ability to understand others is one of my gifts. It doesn't make me better than others, but it's a big part of the best me.

When I first took the Myers-Briggs, I had no idea how much it would change my life. This was a classic example of serendipity: I was looking for a job; I found a calling. I realized immediately that I wanted to become qualified to use the Myers-Briggs with others. After six years of various forays and experiments in the working world, here it was, finally, unexpectedly, like a beacon in the night: I knew what I truly wanted to do, and

I knew what I had to do to get started. Finally, some blessed clarity!

That was seventeen years ago. The road from there to here has had many unexpected turns and obstacles. My ability to deal with those happenings has been immeasurably enhanced by type knowledge. I'm grateful that I recognized—and seized—the opportunity to learn something that would be profoundly useful, not only for myself, but also for others. It is something I enjoy sharing.

There was one big surprise lesson along the way: humility. Learning the MBTI® was challenging, but doable and interesting; it was something to sink my teeth into. Learning to start a consulting business was something else altogether! It required accounting and marketing skills I neither had nor particularly wanted to have. I had to learn to make cold calls and convince people that I was a miracle worker. There was no one to guide me through these uncharted waters. Predictably, given my insecurity, it was easier at times to procrastinate. Of course, that only reinforced my feeling that the challenge was impossible and heightened my sense of abysmal failure.

Tired of false starts and lack of response, I almost quit consulting several times. But Destiny didn't have that in mind for me: every time I got really close to giving up, along came a job opportunity and a another chance to do something I love and believe in.

Over time, I have come to realize that the difficulties were blessings in disguise. When success comes too easily, our egos can go seriously awry and lure us into thinking superior thoughts, invincible thoughts, arrogant thoughts. We start to believe we are something extraordinary or special. I haven't enjoyed the times I've had to walk away from potential contracts without a commitment, but those experiences have humbled me. As I look at other people's efforts, I am more tolerant and more aware of how fragile we all are and how much we need to be kind to one another. I suspect I would be less aware of those things if my business had come along painlessly. Every experience has something to teach us. Our job is to be open to the lesson.

My Dorothea Imbroglio was a very difficult time for me. I teetered on the edge of depression, unsure of how I could follow my bliss without screwing up everyone else's. I knew that my husband and children were my most important priorities. I knew that whatever solution I concocted for myself would have to preserve the conventions and traditions we had come to value in our life as a family. What I didn't know was how I might put all those things together in one compatible package.

The anonymity of being "entangled in the ordinary" sometimes overshadows and obscures underlying possibilities. Our tapestries blur before our weary eyes. We get lost in the "knots" and are unable to see the "threads." We see messy panels in shades of gray, lacking the colors that would define pattern and meaning. In such times, we need to figure out how to clear our vision, focus on individual threads, and weave our circumstances, dreams, and responsibilities into one wonderful, daring, cohesive, joyous whole.

> *Don't compromise yourself.*
> *You're all you've got.*
> —JANIS JOPLIN

I was always looking
outside myself for
strength and confidence
but it comes from within -
it is there all the time.

- ANNA
FREUD

SECOND
MOVEMENT:
Authenticity, Familial and Personal

My Mother,
Myself
and Not Myself

*…the family is the most powerful emotional
system we ever belong to…You might say that our original
family is like a hand of cards dealt by fate. And that our life
task, emotionally, is dealing with this hand.*

—BETTY CARTER AND JOAN PETERS,

LOVE, HONOR, AND NEGOTIATE

The urge to protect and nurture our children is primal. Overall, most parents do the best they know how to do. They struggle with interwoven complexities of finances, family politics, social and cultural agendas, and different personalities. They do this "for better for worse...in sickness and in health." Yet, no matter how much parents "care," children inevitably wind up with a mixed hand of cards. That is the human condition. Even if our offspring get some "aces," undoubtedly they also get some "wild cards" that require neutralization or creative strategy. Bringing life's hand of cards to its best potential fruition is challenging, life-long work.

The effects our family of origin exerts on us are grossly underestimated. Especially when we are young, many of us feel that we can override all that programming and simply be whoever we want to be. That's what I always thought, anyway—and I started with a good hand of cards. Through experience, I learned that my parents' patterns cast very long shadows, indeed. I am only now, at midlife, appreciating how long those shadows are, and how they have distorted and challenged my mission to individuate, to become fully myself.

Ironically, the major challenge in my development as a woman has been my view of my mother. I say "ironically," because I cannot remember ever being really angry with her—ever. I always admired her calm, accepting manner, her "comfort in her own skin," her unselfish acceptance, and her genuine joy in the accomplishments of others. She seemed incapable of jealousy or smallness of spirit of any shape or kind. I respected her intelligence, her indefatigable good humor, and her un-swervingly ladylike behavior. She never so much as raised her voice or let slip a four-letter word. How, then, did this lovely woman present a major challenge?

I knew I could not be her. I am too hotheaded, too opinionated, too willful, and too independent. Although I didn't want to repeat the prac-tice with my own husband, I respected her total deference to my father, assuming it was right for her. Here was a woman who would go to bed when my father did, wait until he was asleep, then creep out of the room to do whatever she really wanted to do in the still of the night. I never found out why she felt she couldn't simply stay up in the first place. I attributed it to the post-Victorian era of her upbringing. In those times, women simply "fit in," accommodated, and lived in the spaces left by the men in their lives.

I thought that knowing this background about my mother's behaviors would give me a feeling of permission to do things differently, but it was not as helpful as I had imagined it would be. Somewhere in the back of my mind, every time I asserted my wishes, the satisfaction of self-expression was contaminated with the guilt of not living up to my mother's saintly example. If I didn't like her so much, it would have been easier to reject her ways. The gulf between intellectual understanding and gut acceptance is very wide, indeed. I remained stalled in those ambivalent doldrums for decades, now edging forward, now falling back, incognizant of what was preventing permanent progress.

Only very recently has the direct mind-gut illumination finally occurred: I've spent my adult life trying to be my mother while also trying not to be my mother. I needed to differentiate the wheat from the chaff, keep the one, and blow the other away. Take what works, let go of what doesn't, and judge not for others. Comparison is not only deadly, it is misleading and counterproductive. We are different beings. One is not better, the other lesser—rather, each of us is unique. The highest honor mothers and daughters can give each other is to be true to themselves. Ironically, this was Mother's earliest admonition to me. Add an ability to genuinely respect "otherliness," and the connections between mother and daughter become very sweet, indeed, bonds replacing bondage.

This is the individuation that is our life's work, and for each of us, the job is unique. Trying to fit into another's mold only prolongs the process. In her book *Love, Honor, and Negotiate*, Betty Carter recommends drawing up a genogram, which is a formalized way of looking at your family tree and recognizing the issues, patterns, and familial themes that are inevitably at work in your life. As a systems-oriented family therapist, Carter contends that we cannot grow into ourselves and into new families when we marry without recognizing and dealing with the issues of our original families.

But how do we get from recognizing what is going on to actually resolving it? Parker Palmer suggests a possibility in his book, *The Courage to Teach*. Referring to teaching methods, Palmer talks about the folly of imposing one way of presenting lessons as being the "best." One passage leapt off the page: "When person A speaks, I realize that the method that works for him would not work for me, for it is not grounded in who I am…" Palmer admonishes me to find methods that "feel integral to my nature." We need to do things in a manner that is consistent with our innermost, true selves, bypassing those methods that, while perfectly logical or effective in and of themselves, are somehow incongruent with our own values. An excellent solution for someone else may not work at all for me. Conversely, just because something isn't good for me doesn't mean it isn't viable and appropriate for someone else. Thus, as we learn to be truly ourselves, we also learn to let others be themselves, thankfully releasing us both from a negative, spiraling pattern of judgment.

How does this play out in the real world? It means that we no longer feel like we have to come up with answers for other people's problems. It means that when my husband handled our grown children differently than I would, after a quick wince, I let it go. I let it be their issue to sort out. It means that I finally understand, with my gut as well as with my head, that my mother is not myself. Finally, I am free to love her, honor her, and enjoy her uniqueness without feeling obligated to replicate it. Finally, I have grounds for true, lasting integrity, which is "the quality or condition of being whole or undivided."

> *You were born an original. Don't die a copy.*
>
> —JOHN MASON

Authenticity Trumps Animosity

It was 1981. The United States was painfully clawing its way out of an era of double-digit inflation. We were a single-income family with two small children, so the inflationary years had been especially hard on us. We were okay; everyone was warm, clothed, and fed, but there wasn't much slack in our budget. It was not a good time to change jobs, but the climate at my husband's workplace had become increasingly confusing and unrewarding. As we explored our options, we decided that the best one would be for my husband to hang out his shingle as an independent consultant in his field of expertise. He would need some help, though, help we could not readily afford to hire. I offered to fulfill the secretarial duties, since it seemed the best way to maximize our profitability. In retrospect, I can see that I was censoring my private reservations. I had zero experience beyond typing papers in college. Besides that, I didn't like any sort of clerical work. However, I figured I could learn what I needed to know, and I wanted to be a team player. Our business was born, and we were partners.

Whew! All I can say is that I genuinely admire couples who work together. Fortunately, we learned to laugh about most of the things we could have shouted about. We made jokes about "the secretary's" poor typing and the "boss's" finickiness. We held "board meetings" in bed. We made creative use of the expense account. Fortunately, my secretarial chores took only eight to twelve hours a week on average. Unfortunately, the first year of my duties preceded our purchase of a computer. (Hard to believe, but only that short time ago, computers were the exception, not the rule.) Hence I often typed almost to the bottom of a page of specifications—the language looked like gobbledy gook—made some irredeemable mistake, and was forced to start all over again. My defenses were varied. Often, I would be overcome with sleepiness, a curious symptom. I would curse quietly, procrastinate endlessly, and berate myself profoundly.

Never, however, did I share my unhappiness with "the management." I felt like I "owed" this service, regardless of my feelings or circumstances. Since I wasn't bringing in any money, I felt powerless. Notice that: I felt powerless. No objective assessment of "power issues" occurred, nor would it have made any difference. I had short-circuited to an intuitive feeling of having no rights, no power.

I never communicated my desire to look for other solutions. I made the decision by myself that there were no viable alternatives. So I "continued to continue," a wonderful phrase from Simon and Garfunkel suggesting dogged tenacity. I became increasingly resentful, and soon my sense of self-esteem and satisfaction had diminished even more than I realized.

Inevitably, of course, the animosity inside the pressure cooker built to the point of bursting. It took two years. Two years! One fine morning, my husband asked some benign question about an invoice I'd typed, and the lid blew off the cooker. It was as if another person answered him, shouting, ranting, raving, crying—totally out of control. I couldn't believe my behavior, nor could I stop it. Poor Jack. He sat there, listening, and finally said, "Where did all this come from? I had no idea you were so unhappy." Neither had I. I had refused to acknowledge being unhappy because I found it unacceptable to feel that way. Denial, however, takes you only so far. Denied feelings have a way of seeping out in other places, creating insidious, unpredictable results.

A painful conversation followed. It was painful because I wanted to be perfect, and clearly, I was not performing to the standard I had set for myself. There was another result, however, an unexpected one. The world did not fall apart. My husband was not angry with me, only concerned and frustrated that I had not shared my point of view sooner. "How can I trust that you are telling me what you think? What you feel? What is authentic?" he asked.

The answers were not immediate. Rather, we had begun a long over-due conversation. The first illumination was that shared frustrations usually lose a significant degree of their intensity, just in the act of sharing. We feel so much better about ourselves when we are being honest. Ideally, we manage to be honest before we reach the powder keg, graceless stage of communication, but even an outburst leaves us feeling better than it feels to simmer inside with the vitriolic poisons created by lying to ourselves.

I realized—and must re-learn this lesson often—that there is no peace without authenticity. Authenticity does not give us license to step tactlessly on other people, but neither does it require us to be something we're not. The road to authenticity is assertive communication. Assertion is honest and direct, an appropriate means for expression of emotions, feelings, and opinions. It opens the door to objective negotiation, which in turn allows for finding win/win solutions.

In time, we decided together that I needed to pursue my own talents and dreams, which created a new, scary problem: figuring out what those dreams were. Jack's circumstances also underwent a major change, and he returned to a corporate setting. No more bedroom board meetings! A buffet cabinet replaced the "secretary's corner" in the dining room. I had my days to myself. Nonetheless, the lessons learned from this cooperative venture were of incalculable value. We can be flexible. We can stretch, do different things, find unusual solutions. We can learn to be honest. Indeed, it is only when we learn to be honest that we are truly empowered to make the best decisions and plans.

Alas, no matter how brilliant the illumination, we never seem to get totally beyond falling into the same, familiar traps now and then. What I do know is that any time I am fighting off hostility or animosity that I just can't seem to dispel, generally the problem is that I am not being true to my authentic self. And that, in the end, is our only responsibility: to be who we are.

> *Never, "for the sake of peace and quiet,"*
> *deny your own experience or convictions.*
> —DAG HAMMARSKJOLD, *MARKINGS*

When Doing Things Your Way Is Self-Sabotage

I did it my way…

—POPULARIZED BY FRANK SINATRA

We've all been there. Our husbands, or for that matter, anybody, offers to do some household chore, a chore that has customarily been our personal bailiwick, and soon we have a dilemma. I could say much about how job descriptions get assigned in the first place and how the very concept of "helping" may in itself illustrate a larger problem, but here I want to focus on authenticity and offer a caveat about avoiding potential self-sabotage.

And so, when the offer of help comes our way, creatures of habit that we are, we are caught by surprise. Not that these "nearest and dearest" aren't helpful in many of their own idiosyncratic ways, but we are ever so pleased that something has moved them to say, "I'll clean the kitchen tonight."

Then the fun begins, as they proceed to do the chore according to their own standards and logic, perhaps throwing out what we would have saved for lunch, neglecting to rinse plates before putting them in the dishwasher, or using the wrong kind of cleaner on a Teflon-coated pan. We fuss, correct, and instruct; and then we wonder why they never offer to help again.

If you're like me, you do this kind of thing at times without even realizing it. You get caught up in your own logic, your own way of doing things, and think that "just this once" you'd better manage the project and tell them how to do it. It is so much easier to see the folly of this particular behavior when we observe it in someone else. My wake-up call came from a good friend as I watched her fuss at her husband. Something clicked in my brain: if we want chores to be shared, we must also share control. Husbands and other people we are close to would probably do more if we didn't micromanage the way they choose to operate.

We have a choice, but it means learning to choose our battles. Do we want help, or do we want our own brand of perfection? Chances are, we can't have both. If sharing is our goal, we have to learn to bite our tongues. We have to refrain from suggesting that more fits in the dishwasher if you do it such and such a way. We have to learn to stop interfering with how our husbands discipline the children because we would have handled it differently. We also have to learn to object when those same "nearest and dearest" try to micromanage the way we help with "their" chores.

Division of labor is a big issue, particularly between husbands and wives in dual-income families. Who cooks, shops, and minds the children? Statistics show a slight shift; that is, men participate more at home than they once did, but that shift is certainly not commensurate with the change women must make. Much ado has been made of this. There has been much discussion about male chauvinism, downtrodden women, inequality, and so forth, ad infinitum.

No doubt many of these questions raise valid issues and pose difficult challenges for everyone involved. But change is awkward and slow, and most people tend to follow the examples they had when they were growing up, even when they discount those examples. Since homes in the previous generation were largely the domain of wives and mothers, there are legions of men out there who don't quite know how to make changes, even if they are willing to do so.

There is another side to this issue, however, an identity side. It is because we identify with the jobs we do that we have such a hard time sharing them and allowing others to do them differently. The old do/be dilemma rears its head in yet another place. I line up the canisters and adjust the various kitchen paraphernalia as I finish tidying the kitchen. It is a ritual that has evolved through years of cooking, a loving signature of leaving my workspace the way I like to see it and the way it is handiest for me to use. Fine. And, I suppose, it could be my "privilege" to insist that all these things are left just so. That "privilege," however, carries a consequence: no one else will care to use "my" kitchen and help me do things in it.

We have to learn to accept different standards for different circumstances. When I cook and clean up, I do it the way I prefer to have it done. When others work in my space, I need to look the other way, pour a glass of wine, and remind myself how lucky I am that they have chosen to share this time and activity with me. And then I have to let them do as they please. Well, most of the time. Some things truly do matter and do require intervention, but no doubt most of us tend to overdo in that regard. For instance, if someone doesn't know that you can't put metal in a microwave, it's time to chime in and tell them! Once the "help" is completed, of course, there is nothing to stop us from rearranging things the next time we're back at work by ourselves!

The kitchen, you see, is not who I am. The kitchen is merely a tool, a means to an end. If we women can be clear about this being/doing issue as it relates to control, we can begin to loosen our reins, allow some flexibility and disorder in our lives, and—surprise—even learn to enjoy it! Cultivating a different attitude is the beginning of a whole different kind of freedom. A house—a home—exists to serve the people who live in it, not vice-versa.

Granted, those who share a home need to arrive at some consensus about accepted modes of operation. Somehow, tensions about tidiness and standards of cleaning and other such things that are peripheral to relationships become central when there is not a reasonable degree of agreement among the stakeholders. We have only to think of Felix and Oscar in Neil Simon's *The Odd Couple*. Stories of such incompatibilities are only funny when they are someone else's stories.

Once we've achieved an understanding about the basics, it's freeing and energizing to let go and allow for variety. It's like living on a different plane; it's life with a whole new dimension. The truth is that many of the things we have been tempted to fuss about simply are not worth even thinking about. How much nicer to plunk down in a chair and read or go out and putter in the garden. We don't need everything to be "my way."

This issue of control gets even stickier when it relates to interpersonal dynamics. How about those times when we disagree with our mates about how to handle a social situation or how to discipline our children? What if we think leniency is in order and our husbands pursue the hard line? I'm a bit chagrined to admit that I used to think I knew more than my husband about what was right for our children because I had spent so much time with them, read so much about child development, and had so much experience with children as a former educator. What presumption. What hubris!

The truth is that children benefit greatly from experiencing the outlooks, values, and styles of both parents. After all, they will need to be able to deal with all kinds of people and a great variety of circumstances as they grow up and head out into the world. Often, too, one parent's tendency to emphasize one kind of approach will be balanced by the other's preference for another. I tended to explain overmuch, and my husband understood that there were times when "because I said so" was perfectly appropriate.

Getting up in the morning and anticipating the day ahead takes on a special sweetness when spiced with openness, with flexibility, and with the possibility of chancing upon something new, something different, or something unplanned. Giving up some control invites a certain degree of serendipity and mystery into our lives. There is something about being open to suggestion that feels lovely. Coffee on the terrace? I hadn't thought of it. I have a busy day ahead, but the little extra time it takes to carry a tray into the garden is more than compensated for by the songs of the birds and the sweet smells of fresh air and spring flowers. Should I change my plans because my husband has a sudden inspiration to tackle some house project that needs two people? Maybe so or maybe not, but when I am open to considering it, that sets a very different tone in a relationship, one of give and take, one that invites spontaneity and freshness.

There will be tremendous benefits from cultivating this openness and flexibility as we age. There is a significant chance that someday we may find ourselves unable to totally care for ourselves. We may even find ourselves in a nursing home, as my mother did. We will need to be able to accept other agendas and other ways of doing things. Hopefully, we will be able to give up control gracefully. What better training than to fully recognize our partner's individualities and learn to share control now.

We are not independent but interdependent.

—BUDDHA

Many Melodies, One Authentic Self

Put all together, what do these musings mean? Are we any closer to equilibrium, to inner harmony?

I think so. Each of these lessons is one more baby step forward as we learn first to differentiate between "doing" and "being," and then come to grips with anonymity, ego, and humility. As we begin to see ourselves solo, minus the layers of our family of origin, we find—and dare to pursue—authenticity. Finally, having found authenticity, we can learn to stretch a bit to let others "in." We can let them express their authenticity, as well.

These are the multiple "melodies" of Counterpoint. They weave together to form the complex "compositions" that are our lives. Each "melody" has its own distinct personality and takes its turn at prominence, playing out in relief against the co-existing, contrasting tunes. The thematic fragments remain identifiable even within these complex combinations and somehow hold their own in spite of the many competing voices. They are the bits and pieces of our authentic selves that we have retrieved from our innermost depths. We garner them, weave them together carefully and lovingly, even knot them together when necessary in order to bolster the fledgling self that struggles relentlessly within us, striving to become fully alive at long last.

In his wonderful poem "Keeping Things Whole" Mark Strand reminds us that no matter how complicated the patterns seem, they would not be complete without all the pieces. "Wherever I am, I am what is missing." That is what Counterpoint reminds us: many themes, but only one whole, a dynamic whole that requires us to keep moving, keep growing.

> *Look inside. That way lays dancing*
> *to melodies spun out by your own heart.*
> *This is a symphony. All the rest are jingles.*
> —ANNA QUINDLEN

Improvisation

The art of performing music
as an immediate reproduction of simultaneous
mental processes; that is, without aid of
manuscript, sketches, or memory.

I get up I walk
I fall down

Meanwhile
I keep
dancing.

RABBI HILLEL

You Can Have Anything You Want, but Not Everything

Learn to get in touch with the silence
within yourself and know that everything in this life
has a purpose. There are no mistakes, no coincidences;
all events are blessings given us to learn from.
—DR. ELISABETH KÜBLER-ROSS

It was a winter night. I was on vacation, walking the dog on a lonely beach and savoring the brightness of a full moon and the relative warmth of a Florida evening in the middle of February. Suddenly, clouds rolled in, forming first a filmy haze and then a total blackout. The lovely light, so symbolically reassuring, was gone. "But the moon is still there," I thought. "Those clouds won't last forever."

This is so much like a woman's life: clouds of quandaries, constrictions, agendas, issues, and questions often obscure the many possibilities. The light is always there, however well hidden it may be at any given time. So it goes, round and round. Are there some tangible ways to dissolve the clouds and reveal the light? Is it possible to wade through the mire, find satisfying solutions, and come out whole? Are there watchwords we might adopt when we are floundering so that we can center ourselves? Can there be guidelines to help us find our way to harmony? Are there approaches and attitudes that bestow blessed serenity like a benediction?

Intuition, that insistent, subconscious, underlying voice, hums along, proclaiming, "Love is the answer." But if, indeed, love is the answer, how do you "do" love? What is the method? How does it manifest itself? How do you know when you're on the right path?

Well, you can't always know, at least not beforehand. You need a supply of concepts, paradigms, and ways of thinking to help you during times of uncertainty, ready to be implemented, manipulated, substituted, changed, played with, and even, sometimes, thrown out so you can start all over again.

Musicians have a wonderful process for messing around within concepts to create new possibilities: improvisation. In music, improvisation means making up what you play as you go along, rather than playing notes that composers have written on a page. In life, it means making do with whatever circumstances are at hand, creating actions extemporaneously within the context of now, and being ready to try doing things in new ways.

However, you need to know the rules before you can bend them and go beyond them. You must learn the language first. In music, that means understanding scales, rhythms, cadences, and so forth—the musical "parts of speech," as it were. Then comes syntax: an understanding of the ways these elements may be combined into structural forms and made into combinations of sounds that are pleasing and sensible to the ear. Once you have internalized the language of music and used these techniques until they are as familiar and easy as making breakfast, it becomes possible to use them spontaneously, in new ways, on the spot. You come to the point where you don't need the sheet music in front of you to tell you what to play. Intuitively, you know how to make music extemporaneously. Your own music, springing from deep within, springing from that place that is beyond words and explanation.

In the school of life, you can begin by understanding the "sheet music," that which is playing out in your life right at this very moment. Wherever you are, however you find yourself, this is the sum total of your circumstances and outlook, your present reality. Every day that dawns, you get to choose anew: you can follow the page of sheet music and play what is prescribed, what is already there, or you can recombine the elements by using skills of reasoning, thinking, evaluating, feeling, and so forth. Flexible recombination can help you get out from under the clouds and find ways to get beyond the page and improvise like a master musician, composing your own pathways as you go along.

Admittedly, much of the time you simply play the music on the page in front of you, because that sheet of notes represents a modus operandi that has developed over time, one that has worked for you and gotten you to where you are. Life is busy, busy. Not every situation calls for improvising new ways to do things. It's when life isn't working or when it's dull or unfulfilling that you need to stray from the sheet music and see what alterations you can make. You will only stall and bog down if you keep doing what you've always done while expecting different results. Improvisation takes courage and faith that, if you leap, somehow you will manage to land on your feet. Knowing techniques empowers you to know also when to depart from them and stretch them.

In life, the tools for improvisation are a blend of multiple continuums: stillness contrasted with action, reflection versus commitment, objectivity versus intuition, long view versus immediate view, and assertiveness versus compromise. The foundation holding these concepts together is an abiding sense of faith, self-worth, and forgiveness, as well as the readiness to make course corrections. There are no set formulas for applying these touchstones, but if you look at this list when you're stuck and try what you have not yet tried, chances are you can avoid prolonged derailments. When all else fails, you need to listen for the shout of your inner voice, "Try something else!" The process isn't linear and exact. You will need to feel your way, much as a good improv musician does.

Stillness is a good place to start. We Americans aren't very good at stillness. We get few opportunities to practice it. We are bombarded with sound and sight stimulation everywhere: ubiquitous television, Muzak on elevators, telephones, and radios blaring even at the gas pump. Introspection is underrated and discouraged. And yet, it is only at our silent centers that we can truly know ourselves, grasp our own individual truths, and discover the voice of improvisation that is waiting for an opportunity to come forth and express its inherent wisdom.

There are many ways to learn to be still. None is easy. Industriousness is the great American way; stillness is its very opposite. This is about being versus doing. Serenity may be a byproduct of what we do, but knowing what to do can be accessed only, in the words of the poet E. E. Cummings, through "the root of the root and the bud of the bud" that is found in our inner, core self, a self that is found only in silence. The silence we seek is aware, not restless; it is observant and accepting.

The quest for stillness is in itself a lesson in improvisation. You may have to try many methods before you find one that works for you. Meditation, prayer, sitting quietly, experiencing nature: make it up as you go along. You'll know when you're on the right track because your spirit will tell you via an inner sense of grounding that is hard to describe but unmistakable when it happens.

After stillness: action. The word action is full of energy, forward motion, and doing. How do you know when and how to embrace action? Often, the timing or even the specific action to take is frustratingly unclear. After inactivity—especially if you have been able to become still, to go inside yourself—it is time to act. "We cannot direct the wind," as the saying goes, "but we can adjust our sails."

Related but not identical to the stillness/action continuum is the line between reflection and commitment. Reflection is stillness turned to deliberate contemplation. Where stillness observes, reflection considers. Commitment then becomes the catalyst that turns reflection into action.

Stillness teaches us to listen. Stillness says, "Accept what is, including yourself."

Reflection says, "I accept what is. What is the best response?"

Commitment says, "I've considered. I've weighed the available information. I've chosen a response, and I will implement it."

Only then are we ready for deliberate—not reflexive—action. There are subtle differences among these processes, but each is necessary in its own way as love unfolds from our inner beings into our outward expressions.

Years ago, I was discouraged, depressed, and agonizing about what to do with my life. I spent months, perhaps years, wringing my hands and allowing my mind to drift aimlessly over random possibilities. Stuck, I realized I had to come to a point of stillness before I could move on.

The following Zen koan points out the importance of getting beyond interior noise:

A professor went to Nan-In, a Japanese master, to inquire

about Zen. As they chatted, Nan-In served tea, pouring his visitor's cup full, and then pouring more, until the cup was flowing over. The professor watched until he could no longer restrain himself. "It is overfull. No more will go in," he exclaimed.

"Like this cup," Nan-In said, "you are full of your own judgments, opinions, and speculations. How can I show you Zen until you empty your first cup?"

Only when we "empty our first cup" will we be ready to reflect, with our eyes trained on the future and not on the past. Silence—which at times can feel more like a frightening void than like stillness—is the beginning of discovery, of seeing what is inside. Rather than repeated random wanderings through ideas long buried inside, we can begin to focus on what may lie ahead. Only after we have come to stillness, to emptiness, are we ready for new things, new possibilities, and the possibility of improvisation.

Improvisation is defined as "making do with whatever materials are at hand, creating extemporaneously within the context of now." During that time of upheaval, I thought about going to graduate school to study marriage and family counseling. Although I came close, I never carried out that plan because the pieces didn't quite fit together to form a cohesive whole in the "now." Cost was an issue. Childcare, time commitment—such hurdles seemed insurmountable. I needed more touchstones so I could see satisfying, viable options beyond this morass of seeming impossibilities.

I realized that I was relying on an intuitive, emotional point of view when what I needed were facts to make productive rumination possible. I needed concrete, detailed, quantifiable information to go along with my feelings and emotions. I calculated costs precisely, brainstormed various scheduling scenarios, and considered specific alternatives for children and family obligations. Only then was I able to return to silence productively. Replacing generalities with specifics allowed me to recognize my truth.

One thing I realized is that it is easy to long for tomorrow and forget to savor today. In the silence of my heart, I knew I didn't want to miss my children's formative years by being preoccupied with a graduate-school

program. Lively, engaged children were the present, immediate situation—
the now. Any solution would have to accommodate this reality. "Remain
in the nowhere else," asserts the Zen saying. "Be here."

Nonetheless, I also needed a long view to go with that present reality. With a far-sighted lens, I began to comprehend—to know in my gut
as well as intellectually—that my children would grow up and all too
soon I'd be on my own, time-wise. There would be other times for other
dreams.

The crux of improvisation, the way that theories transform into
solutions, lies along the assertiveness/compromise continuum. When
you are assertive, you are able to state your feelings, needs, and wants
clearly and respectfully. When you compromise, you settle differences by making concessions. The continuum between assertiveness
and compromise is the range of possibilities that lie between achieving
all of your assertively stated goals and compromising to the point of
achieving none of them.

Sometimes you may unconsciously link an amorphous longing with
some specific action plan, thinking that the plan is what you want, when
in reality, you are trying to satisfy an underlying, perhaps even uniden-
tified, longing. I thought, for instance, that I wanted to go to graduate
school when what I really wanted was involvement. I wanted to deal with
people and interactive processes. These revised, more specific terms, revealed countless new ways to achieve my goal, and many of them could
readily coexist within the other parameters of my life. Being a marriage
and family counselor was not the only potential road to feeling useful and
fulfilled; it was merely the first option I thought of.

Discovering the motivations behind your ideas opens up whole new
ways to look at problems. In my case, I realized that it wasn't a matter of
graduate school or nothing; in fact, there was a whole range of possibilities
between those two extremes. Compromise is the art of seeing how close
you can come to satisfying core motivations while you negotiate your way
along the continuum of realistic possibilities. Fewer concessions may be
necessary if you are able to strip away the outward plan and look beyond
to the underlying goals.

It was important to me to believe that I could have committed to
graduate school. I could have made it happen. On closer examination,

however, the graduate-school plan would not have fulfilled my goals. It felt like a compromise to put that plan aside, but since going to school would not have accomplished what I wanted to accomplish within parameters that were acceptable to me, assertive action required a different tactic. Figuring out the authentic objectives behind this supposed solution allowed me to reframe my thoughts.

The core truth, that I was looking for involvement, was there all the time, just waiting to be discovered. All it took to reveal it was a combination of stillness, reflection, commitment, action, objectivity, intuition, the long view, awareness of the immediate circumstances, assertiveness, and compromise!

It wasn't a solution, but it was an important stepping-stone on the way to finding one. I wanted everything; that was my problem. I wanted a meaningful outlet that could be provided by "work," which I defined as employment outside my home. I also wanted a family, musical participation, volunteering, artistic endeavors, reading, boating, time with friends, exercising, cooking, cleaning, correspondence, and the like. During this round of deliberations I happened upon this thought: You can have anything you want, but not everything. I have noticed that we hear what we need to be thinking about. The content is always there, but we hear it only when we're ready. Spirit is always trying to reach us, help us, and guide us.

Anything, but not everything: I wondered how this applied to me. You can have anything, really, if you are willing to pay the price. That's the rub. If you want too many "anythings," you will find yourself lacking some of the necessary currencies to pay all those prices at the same time. I got it. Choose. You can't have it all, at least not all at the same time.

This is not to say that I gracefully absorbed this realization, smiled serenely, chose a certain path, and proceeded to live happily ever after. Not at all. I was uncomfortable. I wasted energy whining. I even flirted with blame, self-righteousness, and martyrdom—the whole gamut of unproductive behaviors. Finally, I got tired of negativity and came to a point of trying to figure out how to work within my parameters. The most promising and positive possibility that emerged was that I could deliberately choose an overarching approach for achieving overall balance.

Perhaps I could do most if not all of the things I wanted to do if I did them in phases: overall balance instead of immediate balance. Big-picture thinking restores a sense of equilibrium by revealing the possibility of balance over the long haul. Picking and choosing, and knowing that choices can change, helped me feel satisfied in the moment. Because I had considered the options and come to understand how they fit into my sheet of music, I could commit intentionally to family priorities, knowing that while I could pick times for some of my interests, I either embraced the family option when it existed or it would be gone forever. Other goals were potentially more flexible. "Work," though, that unrelenting calling to contribute something meaningful, remained the most challenging of the aspirations to integrate into a bigger picture.

It's important to put on long-range glasses regularly, because a life lived in phases will certainly seem lopsided at times. Parenthood is the classic illustration of this idea. Babies and children immerse parents in schedules that are laden with the young ones' needs. When you are engulfed in this phase, it's difficult to remember that these needs will change, and all too soon, the nest will be empty, leaving you time for other pursuits. Balance over the long haul can also be seen in how things work financially. As much as you try to anticipate expenses and save for them appropriately, during some years, money goes for home upgrades, and during other years, college tuition takes precedence. Exercise and personal pastimes also came in phases: for some years, I played tennis; then I spent years walking; then I spent years biking. Some years, I read voraciously; during others, I found learning a new skill or landscaping a garden more compelling.

Balance is a worthy goal, to be sure, but it doesn't seem to play out that way in real life. Life is not tidy. One remedy for this untidiness is to recognize and list all the variables and all the possibilities. This allows you to make deliberate choices by weighing priorities and needs, check-ing whose turn it is, or evaluating what need should take precedence. Another year will come, and other choices can be made under other circumstances.

And so we improvise. We listen, consider, change, alter, reflect, assert, compromise, and then reflect some more. A few reality checks are useful, too. Spiritually, the African tribal tradition reminds us that, "When you feel good, what you are doing matches your song. When you feel awful, it doesn't." This is an elegantly simple yet profound truth. And it truly can be as simple as that. You can pay attention to what your spirit is telling you, pursue actions that are grounded in who you are, and perform actions that emanate from your essential, if at times inscrutable, inner being. You can trust your intuition, that sublime gift, which was given as divine counsel and sustenance. And you feel good! You feel grounded and have an abiding sense of well-being even through difficult, painful times. Being genuine is the one indispensable ingredient. When your real self doesn't show up for the tasks, everything is a house of cards, ready to collapse with the first challenge that comes along.

To complement the imprecise art of intuition, here is a litmus test for a practical, concrete reality check: Ask yourself if you are falling into the trap of idealizing other possibilities. It is tempting to see options other than the one you have chosen only for their good qualities, overlooking the tradeoffs. You know the problems and frustrations of the road you have taken. You look over at that other road and tend to see only its attractions while remaining oblivious to the potholes that inevitably exist over there, as well. To make sure you're not falling for the "other is better" cop-out, it is a good idea to ask what those downsides might be.

Serendipitously, this idea came to me just before I left teaching to be home with my baby daughter. I was working as a choral director in a large city high school. I had a dream job, directing three choirs and teaching three music classes to a combined total of one hundred seventy-five students. During that era, keypunched computer cards—one per student per period—were the common means of tracking attendance. Those cards were the bane of my existence. I lost them. I sorted them incorrectly. I mixed one period's cards with another's. And I detested the intrusion they made on my time. Nervous at the time about leaving the work world to stay at home, it hit me one day that, should I get fed up with diapers and tedium as a stay-at-home mom, it might be helpful to remember those keypunch cards. They would remind me that, for every choice, there are always downsides and upsides.

There is a final essential component to using improvisation in our lives. If we hope to somehow come out whole and to find solutions that work for us, we will also need to cultivate the ability to forgive. This is not a perfect world, and we, certainly, are far from perfect ourselves. Our judgments, our plans, and our views of others sorely need a dose of compassion and forgiveness to be extended not only to others, but to ourselves, as well. We will make mistakes and missteps. The improvising musician doesn't let a stray note become a problem; he builds it right into the music. We can do the same with unexpected imperfections.

As Buddha observed, "When we hold on to anger it is like grasping a hot coal with the intent of throwing it at someone else: we are the ones who get burned." Forgiveness starts with being gentle with ourselves and radiates outward from there to become forbearance for others. This state of grace doesn't come easily. Our weaknesses and shortcomings hang around and do their best to stop us. Without compassion, however, we are like clanging cymbals: all noise, no grace. Our best efforts are hollow accomplishments, signifying nothing of value. With compassion, we allow positive energy and abundance to replace shortcomings and anger. We make room in our hearts and lives for love in its most complete and essential form. Ultimately, that is the only path to harmony and serenity.

It's wonderful, really, that life is so complex. Yes, it is a burden for us to find our way, but how fortunate we are that our symphonies are so intricate, so interesting. How lovely that there are so many timbres, melodies, and rhythms.

Stillness helps us to appreciate the intricacies, to find the faith to believe in ourselves and in some greater purpose.

Action keeps us involved, actively trying, and ready to adjust.

Reflection centers us.

Commitment is the catalyst without which little happens.

Objectivity adds reason to the gut feelings of intuition.

Somewhere along the way, we need to consider the balance between short- and long-term goals and eventually negotiate our way from assertiveness to whatever degree of compromise it takes to hatch a workable plan. This is a complicated but doable journey. It is sure to be challenging but it is also interesting and rewarding. Taking charge of the process is so much more satisfying than standing by and letting it happen to us.

A soloist has only a few notes to choose from, but has an infinite number of ways to put them together. So it is, too, with life. Ordinary, everyday circumstances may be shaped into many varied patterns as we put the same elements to use in different ways to harmonize our endeavors with the yearnings of our spirits. Empty the cup. Find stillness. Know the rules, and allow intuition to influence how you bend them.

Improvisation is like wind blowing away clouds to reveal a moonlit night. It steers our journey through obstacles and quandaries to possibilities and solutions.

To every thing there is a season,
and a time for every purpose under Heaven.

—ECCLESIASTES

Get up
and out -
the day
is
bursting
with
moments.

TAGORE

Leitmotifs 1

Dominant and recurring themes.

The process
of Living
seems to consist
in coming
to realize truths
so ancient
and simple that,
if stated,
they sound like
barren platitudes.

C.S. LEWIS

Things I Wish I Had Learned Sooner

I would like to learn, or remember, how to live.
—ANNIE DILLARD

"Experience is a dear teacher," said my mother. "Fools will have no other." I was never quite sure just how to take that admonishment, which was one of the few aphorisms she remembered and repeated endlessly into her dotage. Perhaps Mother was simply trying to say that there are many little lessons in life that we don't seem able to learn without direct personal experience. Nonetheless, there is an eternal optimist within me that counter-proclaims: Let's spare ourselves some pain! Perhaps we can be astute enough, attuned enough, to glean the gold from others' discoveries.

Here, then, are some leitmotifs, lessons culled from that "dear teacher, experience." I could have put these observations to good use when I was a young woman struggling to negotiate the inevitable minefields of everyday life. Indeed, I find I still need to remember them again today, as I'm sure I will tomorrow, and all the days after that. Life continues to surprise me with unexpected bumps in the road. These are the watchwords that help me cope with those unavoidable snags.

The term leitmotif is instructive in itself: in Wagnerian opera, leitmotifs were short musical phrases, readily recognizable little mini-tunes that announced important characters in a cast of thousands. They served as tangible aids to help audiences sort out the characters and the plot.

Womansong's leitmotifs are little essays about big recurring themes, themes that are better dealt with when we see them coming and have thought a bit about how to deal with them as gracefully as possible when they arise.

This section, then, written especially for daughters, is also for the recurring, returning daughter in us all, that inner young woman who reappears under duress and stress, unsure, sometimes, of everything. These leitmotifs are touchstones. They are hard learned, hard earned, pithy, and practical, and they guide us when we are under pressure and could use a good short phrase to rein us in and set the proper course.

this too shall pass

We must try to take life moment by moment.
The actual present is usually pretty tolerable, I think,
if we only refrain from adding to its burden
that of the past and the future.
—C. S. LEWIS, *LETTERS TO AN AMERICAN LADY*

The setting: Saturday evening, cozy fire going in the fireplace, candle-lit table set for an intimate dinner for two, Mozart's *Eine kleine Nachtmusik* drifting in the background. As the steaks come off the grill, like clockwork, the baby starts to wail. The new parents look at each other and think, "What have we done? Will we never have private moments again?"

Surely, every new parent hits that moment when the utter euphoria of a new life is replaced by the humorless siege mentality brought on by the unrelenting intensity of caring for a newborn. First you deny it. "I'm just tired tonight." Then you rationalize it. "Of course, I'm annoyed. She's been cranky all day." Finally comes the day when you're just plain fed up and want your life back. This, of course, is followed by guilt, major guilt. "How could I be so small, so immature?"

Back at the Intimate Evening, my husband, much less prone to this guilt shtick, announced that the baby would just have to stay in her crib and cry. We had fed her, she was dry, and it was time for us to have some time to ourselves. I can still see us sitting there in the candlelight, glass of wine in hand, listening to the wails echoing down the hall from the nursery. Dinner was spoiled not only by those plaintive cries but also by a clear disagreement about procedure. Was parenthood always going to be so demanding, so difficult?

After a second glass of wine, my husband said, "You know, this too shall pass. The mistake we are making is thinking that things will always be this way." Of course. Why is the obvious often so elusive?

When you are most discouraged, the problem is not so much the present situation as the imagined permanence of that situation. Almost anything is tolerable in the short run. Long hauls can be much harder to sustain. Interminable difficult circumstances can completely overwhelm even the best of us. The challenge is to become objective enough to assess circumstances realistically. If the source of vexation is fleeting, your attentions can be better spent on finding pragmatic coping strategies. In fact, often the only coping strategy needed is to know that the present circumstances are evanescent, to be gone all too soon, leaving other challenges, joys, and difficulties in their wake.

Let us make a sign, then, one to keep ever within our view as a reality check. Engrave it deeply and beautifully, and embellish it with cheerful flourishes that proclaim the hope of the eternal rightness of things: "This, too, shall pass."

Change Is an Awkward Beast

We cannot direct the wind,
but we can adjust our sails.
—AUTHOR UNKNOWN

I remember a time when I felt like a football player with the ball safely tucked under my arm, running like blazes toward the end zone. Problem was, there didn't seem to be any goal in sight. I was running blindly, not knowing where I was going or why. I kept thinking that if someone would just tell me where—or what—the goal was, my running around could be a whole lot more effective.

My life was in upheaval. My husband was contemplating a job change, potentially one requiring a move to Canada. We had just changed school districts, one of my best friends had moved across the country, and my father had just passed away. With so many changes surrounding me, all I could do was react reflexively. I was too overwhelmed to sort things out rationally and design proactive responses.

Change is an awkward beast, full of stumbles, uncertainty, missteps, and false starts, as well as opportunities. Sometimes change is forced on us by death or when friends move; sometimes we choose it, as in a school change or job change. But whether it is forced on us or we choose it, change catapults us into uncharted territory, and the trip requires enormous amounts of energy, faith, and just plain guts.

Such times are full of mixed feelings. One moment we are optimistic; the next moment, we are afraid of failure. Coming to an irrevocable point of change unleashes tremendous energy. However, self-doubt, lack of clarity, resentment, and even terror may surface at the same time, hampering our ability to move forward. The present is known. No matter how inconvenient, unsatisfying, or unpleasant, we know and understand what we already have. We are familiar with that, and accustomed to coping with it. Change carries with it the nagging suspicion that new "solutions" might actually be worse, a jump from the frying pan into the fire, in effect. Hence, we don't make changes until our pain with the present is greater than our fear of the change we are contemplating.

Often, more than one thing changes at the same time. I suppose this shouldn't surprise us, because most things we do are related in one way or another to the other things we do. Job choice affects where you live, which affects where your kids go to school, which affects your social circle, and so on. The concurrence of multiple big changes, however, can make it very hard to see the path forward and get into a mode of specific action. What we need at such times is focus, a signpost or two to indicate a positive direction. With so many variables, it's likely that those signposts will blur or disappear entirely from sight. The available paths take on the look of a labyrinth, full of possibilities, but also fraught with blind alleys, false detours, and potential minefields.

In our case, the Canadian job opportunity offered promising potential earnings, but also involved isolation from our extended family. Moving would have included the opportunity to live in Toronto, with cultural advantages country people can only dream about. It also would have entailed traffic congestion and acres of asphalt instead of country roads and acres of forests and streams. We didn't know how we'd fare as "city people." It's easy to see how people become hopelessly overwhelmed when faced with so many choices. The temptation to stick with the status quo is an understandable default reaction.

How can you create clarity out of dense fog? How can you gather the courage to move forward when the choices seem so pivotal, so important, and so permanent? You have to start by concentrating on things you can change, and you can't do that until you let go of the things you cannot change. I couldn't bring my father back or influence where my good friend lived. My husband and I had chosen the school change, knowing it was in the best long-term interest for our children's education, even if it was temporarily awkward. Those were givens, and we needed to stop thinking about them.

Even after sorting out the things we couldn't change, the remaining list of decisions to be made was too long to be manageable. Clearly, we needed a corollary to "Concentrate on the things you can change," a way to break the choices facing us into manageable chunks. Concentration, by definition, means focus. We could hardly focus on so many variables at once!

The first step was to make a list of the questions at hand. What about that job opportunity for my husband? What did it mean, not only for him, but also for me and for our children? What other opportunities existed? How could we put together a plan that incorporated the best of the opportunities available to us? How could I help Jack figure out what to do? How could we move on from hand wringing to forward motion?

When you are armed with a list of issues, you need to pick one, any one, and begin. That's the corollary, and it's really that simple. The fear of starting in the wrong place, of making a decision that precludes another, better overall solution later, threatens to derail any forward motion. If factors are interrelated, such as location, family proximity, quality of schools, and climate, and so forth, then it is time to make lists or charts or something to help you see the interrelationships and get a visceral, tangible feel of order, consequences, possibilities, and priorities. More than anything else, you need to realize that very few changes are irreversible.

A letter from an old friend offered a clue about how to overcome this mire of hesitation. She wrote about a problem with her son's schooling and commented that she "kept forgetting how easy it is to act once you set your intention on something." As long as you lock yourself into the "door number one or door number two" quandary, you are effectively paralyzed. Indecision is, in itself, incapacitating.

There comes a point when decisively doing anything is preferable to waiting for life to deliver solutions on a silver platter. Once you start moving, you can begin to sense whether you've chosen the right path. If you haven't, you can undertake a course correction. Reflection serves a purpose, to be sure, but there comes a time to move, a time to do something.

Decisiveness unleashes surprising energy, strength, humor, and self-confidence. It is so much more satisfying to be doing rather than to be hand wringing or dawdling! Curiously, once you start moving, the universe seems to align differently, presenting new raw materials, building blocks, opportunities, and synchronicities you hadn't even imagined possible. It is as if you are living on a whole different plane, wired into a network you didn't even dream existed.

There is an Italian proverb that hints at the power of starting: "For a web begun, God sends threads." This can be hard to remember when you are trying to summon the courage to begin, but there it is: Start! Clarity, help, and all sorts of unforeseen serendipities will emerge as you go along.

Back to the Canadian conundrum: We didn't move. We reinvented a working relationship for my husband. That led to opportunities for professional networking and ultimately to a leadership role within his profession. We also reinvented my role. You could say that my stint as a "secretary" was a disaster. Indeed, at the time, that's how it felt. But that stint was a stepping-stone to learning about who I really am and learning to be honest. Often, decisions are not so much right or wrong in and of themselves as they are right or wrong in the way we proceed onward from them to the next decision, which is a course correction. "If it's not working, do something else," is a common saying. And it is simple, really, although we often refuse to let it be. Lao Tsu reminds us, "The way is simple, but the crooked path is more popular."

It helps to ask what can anchor an impending change or opportunity to those things you value and to the familiar and comfortable in your life. Clearly, the Canadian move did not present sufficient potential "anchors." Not only had we no friends in the area, but we also were strangers to urban living. The money was attractive, but beyond "enough," that's never been a motivating factor for us. In contrast, twenty years later, the North Carolina opportunity presented an intriguing set of anchors. The topography was comfortably familiar: woodsy, hilly, and verdant. The area we found seemed relaxed, informal, and approachable. It was small-town friendly, a milieu we understood. The climate was a Snow Belt veteran's fantasy, with sunshine, moderate temperatures, and a long growing season for all the incredible plants we'd always thought grew only in greenhouses. Most important, from the first hello, the people we met felt more like friends than acquaintances. They seemed to have settled there for the same reasons we were attracted to the area. Instinctively, we felt drawn to the possibilities and sure that we would be grounded in enough similar values to find our way and thrive. Assessing possibilities in terms of values is one more tool for getting out of "stuck" and on the road to action.

Warning: Change doesn't happen in a vacuum. Nothing surprising about that, when you think about it, but often we don't think ahead and consider the ripple effects our changed attitudes and behaviors will have. We are caught off-guard when gripped by a flurry of changes. We have no spare attention for peripheral thoughts, even helpful ones, like the important realization that if we change the way we behave, the people around us will react in new and different ways to our altered behaviors. This can set off a chain reaction of sorts, until no one is sure just why, suddenly, things seem so different, unfamiliar, and out of sync.

We get into trouble with our new behaviors because we tend to make decisions about how we ourselves are going to change and then fail to talk over these situations with the people who will be affected. Worse, we start resenting them for not changing right along with us. Often, these are not conscious thoughts, but even so, the effect is the same.

For example, if you have habitually played the role of accommodator and are one day "illuminated" to become more assertive, it should not surprise you to find your assertion is viewed as rebellion by those accustomed to your usual acquiescence.

As an example, at one point I decided there was no reason that I should be responsible for all the social planning for our family. Nothing wrong with that, necessarily, but I neglected to discuss my changed attitude with my husband. Instead, I simply said, "You make the plans." It's not hard to understand why he saw this as a rebellion and felt threatened by my new, unfamiliar tone of voice.

Ideally, we would work at evolving cooperatively instead of creating havoc with solo decision-making leaps. If I no longer wanted to be in charge of social planning, it would have been preferable if I had found the grace to discuss the matter objectively with the person who would be affected by my change in attitude. And here I must state the obvious: "objectively" does not include ranting, raving, and making accusations. It means a polite re-evaluation, discussion, and request for a new modus operandi. It is an error in judgment to expect people to read our minds and do our bidding without examination, discussion, or consensus. We need to remember that "effective change" has not happened until the necessary communication, negotiation, and realignment of expectations have taken place. Mutually growing into change is synergistic; a solo leap is almost always divisive.

Change itself, then, is a moving target that has multiple players with multiple agendas, multiple moods, and multiple histories. No wonder it is challenging! Sometimes even we ourselves do not notice the changes in our internal attitude. Often, there is a gap between the inward processing and the outward knowing. Although, initially, changes may seem subtle, even unnoticeable, they are often "sea changes," that is, striking transformations. They manifest themselves in external behavior modifications, which in turn ambush unsuspecting souls who suddenly don't know what to make of our strange new ways or how to deal with them.

"This too shall pass" reminds us that many things in life are beyond our control and change without any input from us. "Adjusting the sails" counterbalances this outlook, reminding us that we need to embrace opportunities to choose and to change when they are offered to us. In order to choose an effective course of action, we need to be able to see the difference between what we can change and what we must accept as it is. If you're like me, you wish you had a crystal ball. How easy that would make things, but it is, of course, unrealistic. Reality is much less tidy, and inevitably involves all sorts of miscommunications and misunderstandings along with false starts, aborted tries, and constant course corrections on the road to new and better ways of being and doing.

The journey itself, however, is what is most important. Only by traveling on those highways and byways of change do we "grow into new clothes" when the old ones no longer fit. Each step leads us, ultimately, to the next goal that emerges along the way, like a milepost appearing out of the mist as we inch down a foggy path. Slowly, we become the people we are meant to be. Change is the vehicle of becoming.

> *No amount of falls will really undo us if we keep picking ourselves up each time. We shall of course be very muddy and tattered children by the time we reach home… The only fatal thing is to lose one's temper and give it up.*
>
> —C. S. LEWIS

Facing "Unacceptable" Thoughts

*The biggest handicap women have
in recognizing a need to change is their
tendency to handle "unacceptable" ideas or
impulses by holding them inside, where
they try to dilute them, neutralize them,
take the sting out of them, turn them
into something pleasing.*
—GAIL SHEEHY, *PATHFINDERS*

Reading the above passage led me to an epiphany, a defining, no-turning-back, watershed moment. My everything-is-roses ruse evaporated, and I knew I was not being true to myself. Like Shakespeare's guilty Lady Macbeth who "protested too much," I had been singing too loudly the praises of being a wife and mother and praising too adamantly the glories of family life.

It's a paradox, of course. An important part of keeping a "positive attitude" is to say positive things to yourself, to your family, and to your friends. To some extent, you make your bed of roses by seeing the roses instead of the weeds, by learning to focus on the good stuff instead of the problems. Positive attitude, however, does not mean failure to see the negatives. It means recognizing the negatives, accepting them, and then finding ways to integrate them into a life-affirming vision.

Established formats for writing musical composition mirror this paradoxical truth. Music requires the tension of tonal dissonance in its progression to harmonic resolution. This tension and its resolutions sweeten our satisfaction with what we are hearing, even if we are not conscious of what is going on. So it is with our lives. There are a lot of tensions. Without these defining thoughts and struggles, our lives would be colorless, like lone instruments tooting robotic exercises instead of soaring melodically with the timbres and tensions of the full orchestra playing along.

Certainly, there was a lot about my life that was good, but that was only part of my truth. I also felt isolated and ached with impossible-to-quash feelings of anonymity and inadequacy. Monday mornings came, and "real" people went to work. I stayed home with my baby, piles of laundry, and little everyday jobs that people only notice if you don't do them. Not only that, it seemed like everyone else I knew did those things better than I did. They seemed happier, more on top of things, better organized. Why is it that we are so tempted to compare ourselves to others, particularly when we can't really know how they feel or what their circumstances really are, from-the-inside-out?

I did not allow myself to articulate such thoughts, even inside the privacy of my own mind. I denied them and stuffed them into that blockaded corner of my soul reserved for Unacceptable Thoughts. Like a child with an imaginary friend who does all the bad things he or she would never do, I had this little "not-me" place where I tucked away the negative stuff. Denial, however, is a fragile thing. After I read that single sentence from Gail Sheehy, the blockade disintegrated, and the thoughts burst forth.

I missed my job. I missed being a leader. I missed being listened to and feeling "important." I missed the creative joy of choral directing. I missed my colleagues and my students. I missed freedom. I fought off feelings of being taken for granted. I swallowed my temper when my children stuck up their noses at food I had prepared. I felt odd and defensive about having no paycheck.

Looking back, I see that I was lonely, as well. Not only did I not realize it at the time, I also never could have admitted it. Somewhere deep inside I'd equated even small dissatisfactions concerning my new life as a stay-at-home mom with the possibility that my marriage and family would fall apart. What if I admitted something to myself and there was no solution? What then? Better to ignore that elephant in the living room than chance not being able to deal with it.

Sheehy's book sparked the realization that I had been denying my thoughts by trying to neutralize them instead of facing them boldly and dealing with them. Other inconsistencies came rushing forth, unbidden, unwelcome, but undeniable. They came from everywhere, from family dynamics—the niggling feeling that Daddy was more "fun" than Mommy—to my fear of wind, which is a real problem in a sailing family. In the blink of an eye, I went from carefully maintaining a crafted self-assurance, albeit self-deceptive, to falling apart with diffidence and self-incrimination.

If I'd dealt with these problems as they came along, at least I would have faced them one at a time. As it was, suddenly I felt buried by an avalanche of accumulated negative thoughts and unaddressed problems. What could substitute for the satisfaction I'd found in teaching? Were there ways to "do" motherhood that could fill some of the gaps I was feeling? How could I learn to be less self-critical and stop blaming myself for everything? How could I dispel rather than bury the inevitable resentments that normal children provoke as they fight with each other and test boundaries? Why did I take everything so blasted seriously?

Sadly, disallowing my thoughts to such an extreme degree and refusing not only to think them, but also to share them, robbed those I love of the ability to help me see things more objectively. Jack, my dear, levelheaded Jack, would have been the first to show me the folly—the hubris—of my thinking. Of course I'd feel threatened by the radical change of leaving the "working world." Of course there would be lonely times, as well as ways to combat them. Of course kids will complain about food put in front of them. When you don't share what you're thinking, you develop a sort of convoluted tunnel vision in which you see only part of the picture, which robs you of the objectivity you need to cope, to adapt, and to create an honest positive attitude.

My journal entries show brave attempts that in retrospect look rather comical, rather like painting stripes on a leopard and calling it a tiger. I consciously decided that I needed to feel less guilty and less responsible for everything and everyone. If my kids were unhappy about school or homework, maybe they needed to learn how to deal with the situation themselves. Maybe it didn't matter if the house didn't get cleaned or if I sometimes lacked the enthusiasm and imagination to cook creatively.

I talked to myself a lot about those kinds of things. I spent lots of time thinking about possible resolutions, as if one can decide how to feel and then feel that way. I tried to cultivate flexibility, creative problem solving, and humor. Frozen pizza was always an option. Assigning household jobs could free up my time, not to mention my feeling of servitude. Humor was the toughest: How do you learn to laugh about things you find painful? These were all positive steps, but still suspiciously akin to neutralization instead of to calling a dirty old spade a dirty old spade.

I applied this same tactic of quasi-admission coupled with minimalization to the Wind Problem. Believe me, capital letters are totally appropriate here. I experienced a bad scare early in our sailing days that left me terrified. As my husband and I were returning to our marina in the dark after an evening sail, the wind came up. We broached, meaning that the sail was overpowered and tipped the boat onto its side in the water. Any sailor will tell you that all you have to do is ease the tension in the line to release the wind, and the boat will right itself. That's the cerebral part of the story. The gut part is that I thought I'd never see my children again. It took us another hour or so to reach the marina with no further incident. The damage was done, however; irrational fear of wind had been thoroughly embedded in my psyche.

I was ashamed to admit that I was scared, so I tried, tried, and tried some more to find ways to cope. However, all the positive self-talk in the world cannot dispel real, gut-wrenching fear, because fear is visceral as well as cerebral. Any time the wind would start to whistle through the rigging, my stomach would knot and my normal chatty manner would dissipate into wordless watchfulness. On the boat, I'd yearn for shore. On shore, I'd worry about needing to leave the dock. Once you become engulfed in the physical manifestations of fear, it's hard to convince yourself that there's nothing to be afraid of.

Admission, however, that necessary first step to solutions, was still a long way off. From fear of wind to denial of family life negativities to doubts about my own character traits, I was mired in bogs of self-doubt.

Each "failing," which was what they felt like, tainted the others and made it difficult to sort out the underlying causes and possibilities.

Then, a visit to my family doctor led to a conversation about assertiveness. I do not recall how this topic came up. Certainly, it was unusual. Initially, I couldn't imagine why the doctor would ask me about assertiveness, but he explained that he surmised I was good at asserting myself for everyone but myself. "You come in here and tell me what your children need, but you seem unwilling to talk about what you need." Really? Was I so transparent, and yet so blind? That doctor's kindness inspired me to read about assertiveness skills. His concern gave me the permission I needed to think about myself. It began to occur to me that I needed to see who the "real me" was. I didn't know what I'd find, but censoring unpleasant thoughts had created a false, undependable, unreal miasma that was slowly extinguishing the real me, so I was ready to try thinking in new ways.

For people who have somehow internalized a need for or habit of accommodation, learning self-assertiveness is an awkward experience in which you vacillate between being too nice or too harsh. Slowly, I learned to distinguish the difference between assertiveness (an appropriate expression of personal opinion or want) and aggression (hostile or destructive behavior or actions), which is inappropriate, period. Most of what I'd been struggling with was inside my mind, but here was a concrete, learnable skill that would enable me to begin to communicate those things so that resolutions could replace neutralizations. The beginning of a breakthrough was at hand, presenting clear tasks: look inside, accept what you see, and communicate it honestly and assertively to the people who are affected by those things.

Gradually, I learned to speak my truth—the whole truth. I discovered that my family would not disintegrate if I stuck up for my own point of view. I registered contrary opinions now and then, and the world did not stop turning! I found out that even the occasional cross, nasty, or negative outburst was just that: occasional and unpleasant, but not of lasting consequence. A snit over anything from a messy kitchen to cranky offspring was nothing more that a temporary blip on the radar screen. Why had I ever imagined that a small outburst would become a major calamity?

It took some time to reinforce this new understanding, but slowly I found myself relaxing into a looser way of being. I began to flow more. I allowed a truer, more balanced glimmer of my whole self to come forward. As I expressed myself more honestly, family life started to be more fun, less of a contest. My friendships deepened and solidified. "Real" is so much better than a façade, however "perfect" it may seem.

The biggest challenge remained: The Wind Problem. I still worried about the weather when boating. I think it remained longer than any of my issues because I resisted it the hardest. I resisted it because the stakes were so high: we were a family that sailed! That's how we spent summer weekends; that's how we forged our family's identity; that's who we were. How could I reconcile my fear of wind with those imperatives, those compelling enthusiasms of the rest of my family? We all enjoyed idyllic sunsets seen from the cockpit as we rested happily at anchor in a quiet bay. We loved the early mornings when dawn crept over still, glassy waters, when birds broke our slumber with their songs. We loved exploring the islands, the harbors, and the little towns. I didn't want to ruin this for them. I didn't want to ruin it for me! I didn't want to be left behind. I just couldn't deal with wind!

I wish I could report a tidy resolution, a magic turn of events that solved the problem. Dealing with fear of wind has been perhaps the most difficult challenge of my life. It is ironic, really, that my most difficult challenge turned out to be dealing with the wind—not making a living, getting along with my husband, or any of the usual problems most people would report. And I was dealing with it in the name of pleasure. "Here I am," I remember thinking, "terrified when we are here to have fun." My family knew I became reticent at times and was too quiet and white-knuckled. It would seem to pass—indeed, it often did pass as the wind eased—putting off for yet another weekend an honest discussion about how we could structure our boat time to work for all of us.

Assertively admitting my fear was what finally cracked open the door to conquering my fear. I knew I had to be able to say it out loud. Finally, I came to the point where I could say, "I don't want to go out today. It's too windy for me." All those years I had pretended I was fine had served only to promote mixed messages.

There's an unforeseen consequence to admitting something you've been denying, and you don't discover it until you finally—finally—reach the end of your rope, give up, give in, and speak your true piece. The unforeseen discovery is that admission is freeing. There it is, the worst I've got to give. I laid it out in front of me, naked. And it didn't look so bad, after all! Plenty of people are afraid of things. Plenty, actually, like me, are afraid of wind. It doesn't make me less of a person; it just defines some of my parameters.

There is a corollary here, too, a truism that seems trite, but one not to be overlooked because it is powerful. When you share your fears and your unacceptable thoughts, you actually do lessen them. They hold less power over you because a significant part of the negative energy required by secret thoughts and fears is the energy you use to keep them secret. When you expose your unacceptable thoughts to the light of day and present them assertively to the parties involved, you can begin to use your energies positively and seek resolutions. Fortunately, you don't need to be perfect. It's good enough to be honest and open and keep plugging away at whatever your challenges are.

Thus, ten years or so late, I went off to sailing school. Husbands are wonderful for many things, but often they are not the best teachers for their wives. After sailing school, we bought a different boat, Goldilocks, a charmed lady. She was heavier, less "tender" and tippy, and more solid under sail. She, in turn, gave way to a smaller boat, Loon, and ironically, it was on this little boat that one fine, windy day, my fear just plain went away. Suddenly, my gut caught up with my head. I knew I didn't like a lot of high wind. I knew I didn't care for wild rides and white knuckles, but I was no longer scared. The final irony is that, at that time, we had already decided to sell Loon in order to buy a trawler that we could live aboard during summers.

Perhaps this is a metaphor for life. You have to keep grappling with your fears and negative feelings, yet at the same time, other dynamic forces are at work, changing the playing field, dispersing old challenges, and presenting new ones.

Sorting out these changing situations is an ongoing, life-long chore. No sooner do you get a grip on one set of circumstances than another set comes flying in from left field. You keep thinking that if only you could get past this or that hurdle, you could get on with your life. Odd, isn't it, that we so often view the real tasks of our lives as "interruptions," and maintain some other view, some fantasy, as our personal picture of what our real life is all about. Why is it that, so often, obvious truths simply do not occur to us? Instead, we try to bypass the very struggles that are our mission in life.

There is an irony to the struggle with unacceptable thoughts: because we deny them, we don't know they exist. The struggle, therefore, is not so much to deal with the thoughts themselves as it is to see them in the first place. Unacceptable thoughts probably vary from generation to generation. Young women today might be less inclined to deny the frustrations of new motherhood than I was, for example, but I suspect that all we women, of any age, have them. The insidious power of these unrecognized thoughts lies in their namelessness, which creates tensions we are helpless to resolve until we allow ourselves to let the thoughts surface and until we own them and honor them for what they seek to teach us.

Tensions, in life as in music, are the building blocks for harmony, although they must be arranged, pulled at, pushed, compromised, sculpted, whittled, and fussed over with feverish tenacity before they yield their intricate, marvelous harmonic resolutions. It's easier to create harmony if you know what the tensions are, and you won't know them until you get past denial and neutralization.

Every time I deny myself
I commit a kind of suicide.
—SUSAN GRIFFIN

A crisis
of
confidence
can be
expected
every now
and then.

Caesura

A sudden silencing of sound,
a pause or break.

The heart
I must have
its time of
snow-
to rest in
silence and
then to
grow.

Both Darkness and Light Are Part of Balance

Your joy is your sorrow unmasked.
And the selfsame well from which your laughter rises
was oftentimes filled with your tears. And how else
can it be? The deeper that sorrow carves into your being,
the more joy you can contain.

—KAHLIL GIBRAN

Where can I start on this subject of "snow," fallow time, sadness, bone-wrenching grief? I find myself uncharacteristically inarticulate, curiously without words to begin. Although in other chapters I share personal stories, in this case, the wounds are too painful and too personal to put into words. My heart knows its griefs, and sharing them would open sutured wounds that have, mercifully, stopped bleeding.

Yet, if balance is the goal, we cannot neglect the dark side of the mountain. There is no light without darkness.

Please pause for a moment. Think through your life experiences. Allow yourself to revisit the times when grief or sadness blind-sided you. Perhaps it was a love affair gone awry or a serious misunderstanding with a family member. Maybe you are reminded of the untimely death of a loved one or of a serious betrayal of trust. The possibilities, alas, are endless. But focus for a moment on those times.

It may be that thinking through them will stir a realization: as surely as sorrows come, they also, in time, moderate and soften into new understandings and insights. Sorrows do not destroy us; they do not extinguish our spirits. Remembering this can make the next occurrence easier to bear. Accepting sorrow unlocks an abiding sense that ultimate resolution lies beyond.

What we know: dark times come. Although necessary, we never seek them; rather, they find us, often catching us by surprise. No two episodes are the same; therefore, there are no formulas for scientifically dismissing them or for dispatching a broken spirit so that we can coast along on a tide of oblivious, skin-deep okayness. No way!

We are not meant to ignore broken spirits and torn hearts. Because mending them is such difficult work, it is natural to try to ignore the task, which is the "I'll be better in the morning" approach. But sometimes we're not better in the morning, and that is the spirit's way of telling us that we must acknowledge and honor our pain, ask it what it would have us learn. There is no light until we accept the darkness. Attempting to go over, under, or around sorrows just prolongs the journey; sooner or later, we must go through the sorrows.

Acceptance is the way through—acceptance of pain, darkness, ambivalence, and uncertainty. We come out on the other side humbled, stronger, and with a deeper capacity for compassion. "Trouble never leaves you where it found you," said Robert Schuller, the popular televangelist. "It will change you and you can choose the change."

Ultimately, the only thing you can do with pain is to give in to it. Avoiding it intensifies feelings, which, rather than dissipating them, warps and distorts them. You can't move forward when you are entrenched in denial. You have to become willing to embrace darkness as you would embrace light. You need to feel it, live it, and wrestle with it until it reveals—in its own good time—a road to resolution. This process is natural, necessary, and universal. It can be shared, but not denied. The medieval Christian mystic Meister Eckhardt provides a watchword for the journey: "Truly, it is in the darkness that one finds the light, so when we are in sorrow, then this light is nearest to all of us."

In your darkest hours, may you remember that despair, too, has its place, its function. May you be gentle with yourself, be patient, and be open. Ultimately another door will open and another source of Light will be revealed. In the meantime, your task is to persevere. Dawn, surely, is on its way...

Bein' lost is worth the comin' home.

—NEIL DIAMOND

Incubation Periods and the Bumble Theory of Forward Motion

One does not discover new lands
without consenting to lose sight of the shore
for a very long time.
—ANDRÉ GIDE

Just as silence has a sorrow side, it also has incubation periods, times when you find yourself stalled, stopped dead in your tracks, wordless and unable to formulate so much as a question or a thought. All you know at such times is that you're out of sync; something's wrong—or is it that something's not right? But the gremlin has no face, no name.

My good friend Peggy refers to these as times of "internal combustion." I like that metaphor because it suggests that great action is taking place at just the time when nothing seems to be happening. We can handle pain, unhappiness, angst, sadness, and quandaries. What we can't handle is standing still, being stalled in a parking lot instead of on a road to somewhere. Anywhere!

Incubation, however, is sometimes the only method of finding the road on which you need to be. A slow, largely passive process, incubation is an important part of finding balance. I suspect that our stalled times are times when we are not ready for, or are subconsciously fighting, what must come next if we are to blossom according to God's intentions for us.

In college, I felt rudderless. I was totally unable to discern any preferred area of study. My enthusiasms, like those of a Renaissance man, were seemingly boundless. No "message" appeared in neon lights when I sat staring at the stars, wondering, "What should I do?" Only silence reigned under the stars and in my heart, but I had to do something. There was always a next semester to register for and requirements to meet.

All I could do was bumble along, accepting short-term strategies until long-term alternatives presented themselves. This "Bumble Theory of Forward Motion" has been surprisingly effective. In a sense, it is the diametric opposite of going through problems. The theory is that if you can't name the problem, you start by patiently waiting it out as long as you can and keeping your options open while trying to determine the best direction to take. When the time comes that taking action can no longer be put off, that's when you bumble on. You pick the most promising option and then discipline yourself to look only forward, to the future, and not back, to the past. This was how I became a music major. What I discovered in the process is that each decision changes the locus of decisions to come. So, the seeming state of being stalled is not static, after all. It moves, if subtly, and it has its purpose.

What about the times when there is nowhere to bumble? Times when you feel like you've outgrown your own skin, when you are cranky for no reason, when you are crying without provocation or sleepless or restless? These are the times before a problem has a name, and they are the worst and most difficult times. When you can't "bumble," the only recourse is to give in to the silence and learn to be still. You can only "Stay in the middle until," as the Zen saying goes.

Silence, of course, is not necessarily the same as "still." Usually, attempts to be still are intertwined with inner conversations. When this happens, it is important to find a way to listen. You can use those internal conversations to uncover the message that the spirit is trying to get through to the conscious mind. Writing out such "chattiness" is my best bridge to stillness. When I use my journal to dump my thoughts, stream-of-consciousness style, I become still enough to listen.

In the end, there are no magic formulas, no silver bullets, and no instant answers. Centuries ago, Blaise Pascal said, "The heart has its reasons that reason knows nothing of," as true today as it was in his time. You must balance the scales, sometimes with action and sometimes with stillness. Sometimes you need questions; sometimes you need faith. Knowing which course to take begins with paying attention and noticing your underlying rhythms. Balance is not science, but art—art that you have to make up as you go along. Each day brings a fresh opportunity for discovery, integration, and healing as you create anew.

There is no libretto.
We need wit and courage to make our way
while our way is making us.

—TOM STOPPARD

Let your tears come;
Let them
water your soul.

EILEEN MAYHEW

Leitmotifs II

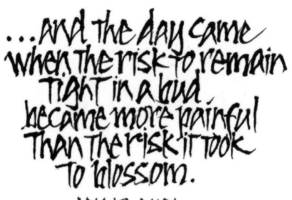

...and the day came
when the risk to remain
tight in a bud
became more painful
than the risk it took
to blossom.

ANAIS NIN

Risk Can Be Healthy

The great affair, the love affair with life,
is to live as variously as possible, to groom one's curiosity
like a high-spirited thoroughbred, climb aboard,
and gallop over the thick, sun-struck hills every day.
Where there is no risk, the emotional terrain is flat and
unyielding, and, despite all its dimensions, valleys,
pinnacles, and detours, life will seem to have none of its
magic geography, only a length. It began in mystery,
and it will end in mystery, but what a savage
and beautiful country lies in between.

—DIANE ACKERMAN, *A NATURAL HISTORY OF THE SENSES*

Risk is defined as "the possibility of suffering harm or loss, danger." No wonder risk carries such a negative connotation! Looking back, however, every Giant Leap Forward in my life occurred because I dared to risk. I wanted to go to graduate school at Harvard University, but did I have the courage to face rejection? The attractive, interesting man I'd met didn't call again after a snowstorm cancelled our date. Could he have lost my phone number, which was in my roommate's name? I couldn't know unless I contacted him, risking rejection. Did I have the nerve to risk a blind phone call when looking for my first post-children job? How could I become a consultant? Would I dare buy the business cards, set up the accounting procedures, and declare myself in business? Could my husband and I move to North Carolina on the strength of an intuitive yearning? I don't think of myself as a risk-taker. Yet none of these remarkable, positive, life-changing events would have taken place without risking the possibility of loss.

Loss of what? What do we have to lose when we risk? Often, the only thing we are risking is the comfort of the familiar. Good or bad, convenient or inconvenient, suiting our needs or grossly violating them, there is some security in the familiar. When opportunities arise and dreams beckon, undesirable consequences are often just as possible as desirable ones. Why try a new business venture when I have a job now with appropriate compensation, great colleagues, and a schedule that works for me? The new situation may look promising, but maybe there's something I'm overlooking. I know what I already have, whereas that opportunity "out there" is an unknown.

There are many kinds of risk, too, as my son has pointed out to me. There is physical risk, like running Class IV rapids down the Nantahala River. There's financial risk; we all know about that one. Although we don't admit to it often, we know about social risk, as well, that anxiety we face when we find ourselves at a party with people we haven't met before or when we're surrounded by people with different opinions and values and feel the need to stand up, be counted, and register an opinion that may not be well-received.

Identity risk is in a class by itself. This is the vulnerable interior risk that involves our core sense of self-image. Do I see myself as a leader? If so, any time I put myself in a position to lead, I risk either reinforcing that image or damaging it. Do I think of myself as a writer? What will it mean if I can't get any of my work published? Would that mean I'm no good? How will I integrate that into my self-image?

Identity risk is the scariest of all, because "failures" attached to our core values are hard to rationalize and difficult to recover from. Alternatively, the "If I haven't tried, I haven't failed" approach makes it attractive to avoid risk in the first place. Hmmm. That also leaves us stuck in the same place, secretly knowing we didn't try, and that's hard on our self-image, too. "Nothing ventured, nothing gained," my mother used to say, but that doesn't necessarily assuage the pain of failure.

On the plus side, and making it worthwhile to cheer ourselves on to risking beyond our "safe" zones, risk-taking is like a growth hormone.

Without it, we live stalled lives, marking time but making little headway. Like pot-bound plants, we survive but we do not thrive.

What is it that enables risk-taking? Indeed, how do we even recognize when hesitation to risk is the factor that is holding us back? On the other hand, running willy-nilly from one possibility to another and daring to undertake any half-baked scheme that appears on the horizon isn't such a good idea, either. We need a yardstick, a way of measuring and comparing the present versus the possible, the status quo versus an opportunity. We also need reality checks to keep us from thinking that every risk is a good risk. Weighing all these parameters concurrently can degenerate into total confusion, leaving us hopelessly ricocheting between, for example, "I should dare to go into business. What's the matter with me? Don't I have any nerve?" and "This isn't about risk; it's about unrealistic ideas."

Once again, a musical metaphor can help you clarify your options. What you need is to quiet the orchestra, slow the tempo, and listen to the ostinato. In music, an ostinato is an underlying pattern that is constantly repeated. In life, it's those core values that define you. You find your ostinato by thinking about what you have to lose by staying in the same place, literal or figurative, in which you are now. While risking change may seem dicey, the pain or dislike of the present may be sufficient to make the gamble of doing something else attractive. Sure, I had a job with predictable hours and okay pay, but those perks paled in comparison to the prospect of sharing important, life-changing strategies with other people, as I hoped I could do if I started my own consulting business.

If you are dissatisfied, restless, or even vaguely discontent, chances are your spirit is trying to get your attention and is asking you to consider another way, another path, or another alternative. It's risky to open that door even a crack; it's risky to even consider the possibility of change. And yet, the first door you have to open is the one that leads to allowing those thoughts. You need to believe that something else can be better and that, if it isn't better, you'll move on and try yet another potential solution until you do "make it better."

Reviewing my turning points, I see how fortunate I am to be a risk-taker. Getting into graduate school was worth the possibility of rejection, because the network and the credibility I gained from participating in that program made it possible to get the jobs I wanted and led to significant opportunities that would otherwise have been unavailable to me. Had I failed to get in, there would have been no consequences beyond the immediate embarrassment of having to share that news with others.

Calling Jack after that initial chance encounter, thinking that perhaps he had lost my phone number, took more courage than I could muster. (What if he were silent? What if he laughed? What if he said, "Who are you?") I was lonely, though, and writing him a casual note was doable. The fact that he lived fifty miles away fed my fledgling sense of bravado. He could ignore my note; I was not going to run into him in the corner store. And it turned out my hunch was right: he had lost my phone number, and six weeks after we reconnected, we were married. Score one for risk!

Note that risks can be leveraged, lessened, or broached at personally acceptable levels. You can choose how much to stretch your comfort zone. Phoning was beyond consideration; it would have been too "forward" to fly within my personal standards of acceptable behavior. The written word, however, offered middle ground: enough distance to feel "proper" without neglecting the opportunity to seize the possibility of karma.

Moving to North Carolina from upstate New York was a huge risk, no question about that. We were tired of long winters. We wanted to live in a small community with cultural and artistic opportunities. We loved the foothills of the Smokies, which were comfortingly reminiscent of the beauty of upstate New York but had a gentler climate. We had a lot to gain, but also a lot to lose: thirty years of friendships and memories invested in upstate New York. Could we keep the best of those friendships and memories yet move on?

It would have been "safer," of course, to take an intermediate step and arrange a short-term rental so we could get a hands-on, accurate picture of life in North Carolina rather than leap blindly, fueled by intuition. Intuition, however, has been kind to us; actually, it has been a comfort zone in itself. We find our hunches tend to "work." This "sixth sense" may not work for everyone, but it has never led us seriously astray. Moving south was no exception.

There are, of course, risks I have decided not to take. I struggle to recall what they were; once a bridge is burned, there is nothing to be gained by looking at the charred remains. What's important is to consider taking a risk, examine potential consequences, and weigh objectively potential merits and the likelihood of their occurring. When you do not actively consider a given risk, you actually gamble something far greater: you may be missing out on a great, life-changing opportunity before it can even begin to blossom and show its promise.

> *…real courage is risking something*
> *that might force you to rethink your thoughts*
> *and suffer change and stretch consciousness.*
> *Real courage is risking one's clichés.*
>
> —TOM ROBBINS

Put Yourself on the List

People are happy helping.
It's never hard to find help.
It is only hard to know it's time to ask.

—MAURICE SENDAK

It's all good and well to talk about assertiveness, read about it, and buy into the concept intellectually. And, yes, it's good to even begin altering your behavior with some degree of self-interest. I found, however, that it was incredibly difficult for me to discern when assertion was appropriate and when I needed to step back, keep quiet, or give in.

The most effective answer to this difficulty came to me, surprisingly enough, through parenting. With two children, I was forever trying to treat them equally, dividing my attention, my time, and our resources fairly. One day, it struck me with incredible clarity: I was a member of the family just like everyone else, and my needs ought to "go on the list," right up there with everyone else's. To the person inside me who was taught to give unstintingly, this made sense and allowed me to think about my needs more objectively.

This concept played out in many small ways that were actually huge. (Funny how the little things often are huge, and vice-versa.) For instance, when I got an invitation from a friend that conflicted with family plans, I learned that I should take stock: Had I had a "turn" lately? Were there other ways to meet other family members' needs that left me free to do what I wanted? More often than not, it was possible for all of us to do what we wanted if we were honest enough to put our wishes on the table and do some creative problem solving.

For many of us, the assertiveness problem edits down to two central issues: feeling worthy, that is, knowing that we deserve our piece of the pie, and learning to ask for what we want.

One unhealthy by-product of the extreme independence that is a hallmark of American culture is the inability to ask for things. Anything! We figure that somehow we're supposed to be able to do everything ourselves. We don't want to owe anyone anything. Hence, we go out of our way to rearrange a schedule when, truthfully, a neighbor would have been all too happy to pick up our child from daycare. We dread asking for a schedule change at work. We even hesitate to ask family members to adjust their plans to accommodate us. We plot and plan our way through the ever-changing maze of details figuring it's our problem to make everything work.

There's some value in this. Most of us have experienced the rude, tactless person who is only too glad to ask for everything, all the time, with no regard for anyone else's needs. As with most things, balance is the issue. My mother used to say that we deny other people the pleasure of being needed and helpful when we doggedly insist on doing everything ourselves. My mother further said that we often don't get to return favors to the people who gave them to us, which doesn't matter as long as all of us are busy passing favors on and on, wherever they are needed.

And yet—and yet—we still hesitate to ask. At least I do. However, not asking is making the assumption that others know your needs and don't care to help. The job, then, is to learn to ask with equanimity, ready for honest answers in return. The case for asking is presented simply and powerfully in *The Aladdin Factor*, by Jack Canfield and Mark Victor Hansen. You might be tempted to dispense quickly with such a mainstream, feel-good kind of self-help book. I certainly was. I read it because I was working in human resources at the time and thought it might "help my clients." Clients, indeed. A quick reading showed me how little use I made of the gift of asking. Sometimes, afraid of rejection or too proud to ask or unable to articulate a just-evolving thought, the request would die in my throat, unspoken, indeed, often unrecognized. We absorb the injunction for independence without knowing we are doing so. It takes focused intention to turn that around. You have to recognize what you are doing and vow to venture forward in a different direction.

Womansong, this very book you are reading, is perhaps my greatest personal testimonial to the power of asking. I have long admired and collected Renée Locks' art and calligraphy. One day as I was sitting at my computer, I stared off into the shadows of my desk, searching for a word. My eye fell on one of Renée's cards that I keep close by to inspire me. "This book needs her art," I thought. And then I remembered Aladdin, admonishing me to ask. I flipped over the card, saw an address, and sent a letter "out to the universe," telling Renée about *Womansong* and my dream that her work would be included in it. Six months later, I heard from her, just one day before finishing the first draft, which was the deadline I had arbitrarily set for looking for someone else if I didn't hear from her. We got acquainted through e-mails and finally met six months later. It was immediately apparent that we were kindred spirits, but we never would have discovered that if I had not asked. Trite, but true: nothing ventured, nothing gained. "Ask, ask, ask," says Aladdin. Ask politely, appropriately, and be ready for refusal as well as acquiescence, but ask.

It is important that we do not unduly inconvenience people, of course, but if we have trouble asking for things, probably we will never be guilty of asking too often or too much. Asking my daughter to change her vacation plans to fit our convenience for a family get-together would be inappropriate. Asking her if she has any suggestions for making both her plans and our collective wish for a family reunion possible is honest and potentially problem solving, an example of healthy assertiveness at its best.

We need to look at ourselves honestly and realistically. Are we reciprocating? That is, are we responding to others' requests as well as asking for ourselves? Are we willing to stretch, flex our mindsets a bit, and abandon today's to-do list when a friend calls needing a ride to the doctor or an unloading-over-a-cup-of-tea commiseration?

Balance means that we are both giving and asking. Giving and receiving form a sublime union. When we ask to receive something, we simultaneously give someone else the opportunity to feel useful and wanted, which feeds the cycle of positive energy flow.

Healthy assertion, then, starts with personal honesty, with willingness to acknowledge your thoughts: noble, ignoble, or otherwise. Pretending not to be thinking about something that is on your mind only muddies a situation, adding layers of denial instead of uncovering and clarifying issues through direct confrontation. Acknowledge thoughts, objectively assess their merit, put them on the list if they are valid, and make your wishes known to the universe. This is how miracles begin!

> *Ask and it shall be given unto you.*
>
> —*MATTHEW 7:7*

(But be careful what you ask for—you just might get it!)

If you don't run your Life, somebody else will.

JOHN ATKINSON

When in Doubt, Slog On...

Just put one foot in front of the other...

—KERNEL OF WISDOM

COURTESY OF AN ANONYMOUS FELLOW AIRLINE PASSENGER

We've all been there: the wonderful trip that disintegrates into a series of delayed flights, missed connections, and other unforeseen complications. In my experience, airline travel either goes like clockwork or goes completely to hell in a hand basket. Once things start to go wrong, typically the whole plan disintegrates, and you're in for a long, frustrating day with who-knows-what consequences.

On just such a day, while in a plane parked indefinitely on the tarmac at the Honolulu airport, I struck up a conversation with my seatmate. She was a lovely woman, friendly and outgoing. The conversation turned, as often happens with women, to our families, children, and jobs. Hers was a tale of woe: she had been widowed young with three children and was ill equipped to deal with being a provider. Woe, however, had been transformed into creative coping, imaginative solutions, and a measure of joy and contentment.

"How," I inquired, "did you manage?"

"You just put one foot in front of the other," she replied. "At first, everything is a blur; you don't know what to do or where to turn. But you do know the kids need to eat breakfast, so you get out the cereal and milk and put it on the table."

A long, fascinating discussion followed. This woman's tale was one of incredible courage, but I was most intrigued by her approach, and it has served as a touchstone for me several times in the years since that conversation. I am a plotter and planner. I like to know what I'm going to do and how I'm going to do it. There are times, however, when no amount of planning can help me, times when I need to simply respond to whatever is directly at hand, putting one foot ahead of the other, and let the next step appear in its own time. What a serendipitous gift to receive in the midst of foiled travel plans!

Perseverance is not a long race;
it is many short races one after another.

—WALTER ELLIOTT

Things Work Out!

It was a Friday afternoon, and I was frantically finishing a work project and trying to gather and pack a weekend's worth of clothing and food for the boat, all the while keeping an eye on the clock because I had to pick up the kids from school. The weather forecast was ominous, threatening gusty winds and thunderstorms. I struggled to stay in positive mode and avoid the temptation to foresee only the worst possible weather scenario. The phone rang.

It was my mother, warning me that the world was going to come to an end that weekend. Seriously! I listened politely. My mother was not a religious extremist, but from time to time she seemed to get caught up in religious prophecies. There was no point in arguing with her or in doing anything other than thanking her for calling. Any other response would have elicited all sorts of hellfire and damnation speeches that, first, I didn't have time to listen to, and second, I had no stomach for.

I hung up, sat down, took three deep breaths, and, looking skyward, wondered what to make of the collection of negative thoughts that were closing in on me. I simply didn't have enough strength or energy to worry about the world coming to an end when I was scared to death of the weather forecast for the weekend. At that moment, I made a decision: I would no longer worry about things I could not control. This was not a new revelation, certainly, but there is a difference between knowing something in your mind and experiencing it in your gut. This was gut-level: "I can't do this anymore." Things would just have to work out as they were intended to, and somebody else would have to be in charge. I was tired, scared, and unable, in those wonderful words from an old Simon and Garfunkel song, "to continue to continue."

I never told anyone about Mother's call. I was too ashamed of how much she had frightened me. We went to the boat and spent a weekend that was memorable only because it was so ordinary. Nothing happened. Mornings still came, weather came and went, and the family made a group decision about the cruising plan that compensated for the weather. I survived, and so did the world. I never had the nerve to ask Mother what she thought about her unfulfilled prophecy.

I have given considerable thought since that day to how I respond to fear. I also tried to understand the role that control plays in my behavior because, intuitively, I sense that fear and control are related. I suspect we try to control things in order to prevent or dispel fear, since fear has a way of derailing our normal coping strategies. We try all sorts of intricate schemes and plans with quixotic tenacity, sure that we'll be able to keep our dreaded fears off our backs if we try hard enough.

Inevitably, we come to a roadblock sooner or later. There is something we fear that we cannot control, no matter how hard we try, and it's not going to go away. Here's the problem: even if I can think the right thoughts, do the right things, and perhaps even manage to hold my feelings in abeyance, my physiology will betray me every time because I can't control the butterflies that nose-dive willy-nilly inside me. They send disquieting messages back to my mind, which unsettle my carefully crafted attempts at equanimity. Like cascading dominoes, my neat little theories and schemes tumble down and fall apart, one after the other, leaving only cold fear in their wake.

Barnes Boffey discusses how we react to fear in his book, *Reinventing Yourself*. He suggests that we can find ways to meet our personal needs within a given situation. Boffey explains how these needs can be tangibly translated into thinking, feeling, action, and physiology through the use of proactive visualization. In other words, if you can envision what is ideal, you can unify your efforts to make that vision into reality. This is "act as if" behavior, and it can be surprisingly effective.

Well, sometimes it can be, that is. At least it helps, but only when the basic fear has been acknowledged first. In my case of fearing that wind would capsize the boat, the only way to even begin to turn the problem around was to admit it. I needed to give voice to the fear, so that some action plan could be hatched to overcome the irrational thoughts that, in turn, set the butterflies in motion. Giving fears a voice is how you begin to have power and influence over them, how you start to find ways to bring them under control.

Why, though, was I so fearful in the first place? Certainly some of my fears relate directly to scary experiences. That's normal and healthy. Also, I believe motherhood changes one's comfort level concerning risk. Children need mothers. I needed to take very, very good care of me to ensure that mine would have one! I got in the habit of being careful and conservative, which is good, of course, at least up to a point. But I seemed to forget how to experience any sort of freedom because I was cautious far beyond reasonable prudence.

Why did I do that? I surmise it is because I was acutely sensitive to the fragility of life. I tried to hold that fragility at bay, to control it, rather than accept it and work within its parameters.

We muddle through as best we can. We attempt to be honest about our feelings. We try specific coping strategies and are as creative as we can about dealing with Scary Things and Unexpected Challenges. As much as these efforts help, it is not possible (at least for me) to believe and live the mantra, "Things work out," unless I add the element of grace: the divine love, protection, and sense of the ultimate rightness of things bestowed freely on people by God. Grace fills the gaps, picks us up, and gives us the courage to keep going, to start again, to keep seeking, to keep trying to be the best selves we can be.

I say this in the broadest, most non-dogmatic, non-sectarian sense possible. The atrocities committed by the zealously "religious" in our world leave no taste in my mouth for dogma. God must weep at our smallness. Yet God—whatever vision of Greater Power or Prime Mover we may hold in our minds and hearts—God is larger than our theories, our philosophies, or our tidy little religious conventions. God is spiritual, ethereal, and not easily quantifiable or reducible to a single, simple formula. God offers grace constantly, and in abundance. It is visible not only in the beauty of this world but also in mysterious synchronicities, happy coincidences, and many small acts of kindness that are evident everywhere if we are tuned to the right frequency.

Some years ago, Billy Graham's newspaper column addressed a woman who was questioning God's presence in her life, which was filled with problems and unhappy situations. Graham asked her to look at her life as a tapestry. He suggested that perhaps she was seeing the tapestry from the back side, where the strands are knotted together and where the overall pattern, beauty, and rightness of the design is not obvious. That image has stuck with me. My tapestry doesn't always make sense from my view of it, but I have to believe there is another way to see it. My life is unfolding and coming together as God intends. The knots lead to something yet unknown, but purposeful. There is great comfort and energy to glean from a basic philosophy that "things work out." For, as Boffey says in closing his book:

We are not human beings going through a spiritual experience, we are spiritual beings going through a human experience.

—D. BARNES BOFFEY

The birds of worry
and care
fly above your head.
This you cannot
change.
That they build nests
there. This you
can prevent.

—MISTER LUI

Fantasia

Free flight of fancy prevails
over contemporary convention of style and form.

I have decided
to be HAPPY
because it is good
for one's health.

VOLTAIRE

Lighten Up!

Angels can fly
because they take themselves lightly.
—G. K. CHESTERTON

"Lighten up!" said my good buddy Marcia, time after time after time, as I'd agonize, wince, fester, worry, plot, plan, stew, and cogitate. "Lighten up!"

Like so many aspects of personality, intensity has both its brighter and darker sides. Intensity can be stick-to-it-iveness, the gumption that gets things done. It can be passion, the prime mover of many a cause. Intensity can be colorful and refreshingly honest. Alas, it also can be obnoxious, unrelenting, pious, and humorless, which is where intensity definitely loses its charm.

I am, however, indefatigably intense. I can't help it. I try to tilt windmills with shocking regularity, tempted by causes of all sorts and descriptions. I "care," and all too often that means that I succumb to the temptation to bend any unwitting but available ear about my current cause. Keeping intensity in check is an ongoing challenge for me.

Enter humor. Humor has a cathartic, leveling influence on intensity; it softens its shrill edges, eases tensions, and opens possibilities. Piety, false pride, and ego go out the window as laughter comes in.

Perhaps the greatest of humor's survival tools is the ability to laugh at yourself, to see—and to accept—your own idiosyncrasies, faux pas, and calamities. Being able to make fun of ourselves makes us more human and approachable. I could have expired from embarrassment when our mortgage officer, showing up unexpectedly for a routine inspection while our house was under construction, found me disheveled, swollen-faced from dental surgery, and poised with a shotgun in the master bathroom (to kill a woodchuck in the garden—what else?). It was far more productive to see the humor in the situation.

It is harder, at times, but so helpful, to conjure up *MASH* humor, so named for the movie in which wartime medical units made fun of the absurd, the painful, and the unspeakable as a means of coping and staying sane. This black humor, far from being irreverent, helps to get us through the calamities, the ironies, and the great sadnesses of life. It's what helped me to laugh (if only on the inside) after my father's death, when, during calling hours at the funeral home, a real estate agent put her hand under the flowers on his casket and asked my mother about lowering the price on the family home. The question needed to be asked, I'm sure, but the agent's timing was unspeakably tasteless and insensitive.

Thankfully, my reaction was humor, not anger. I knew, somehow, that my father was kicking up a rumpus inside his casket, for he detested shoddy, snake-oil-type salespeople. Instead of crying hysterically or yelling at the poor woman, I chose to share a temporally unbounded laugh with my father about the farce playing out in that somber scene. For sure, we set the agent straight and showed her to the door, but the ability to see comedy in the situation made it easier to bear.

MASH humor—laughing at something that isn't actually funny—also took the edge off when I inadvertently backed the car through the garage door. "How can you 'inadvertently' back a car through the garage door?" my husband asked. For a windmill-tilter who was embracing all kinds of schemes and causes, Don Quixote-like, it was easy. My mind races ahead of where I am. I may need to cultivate staying in the present, but there's no sense making a big fuss when I do something dumb. Laugh, clean up the mess, and move on; it's so much easier on me and everyone around me.

Humor starts with you and moves outward, like a ripple on a pond. Poking gentle fun at yourself can be a means of lessening tensions, for it sends a message that you, too, recognize your own eccentricities. You, too, know there has to be room for other points of view. In a meeting, when I speak out too often or too intensely, an, "Ooops—sorry. You know me: Miss Mouth is off and running again. I'll pipe down," can be an invaluable way to re-set the tone and help others to lighten up, as well.

Once you learn to laugh at yourself, you begin to take other people a bit less seriously, too. You discover that sometimes you can choose laughter instead of offense. You can intentionally choose to avoid taking things personally. For a small example, if I choose a DVD that others are not enjoying, that isn't a reflection on me, that's an opinion about a movie.

We need to give ourselves permission to laugh at the absurd, while being careful, however, to avoid denigrating others. We can cultivate the art of light-hearted joking while taking care to avoid meanness and belittling deprecation that puts others down to raise ourselves up. We can learn the effectiveness of cajoling in place of preaching. Attitude is a choice, and we can learn to choose humor and good will.

Some years ago, when our children were teenagers, my husband and I were annoyed by their constant excuses. One day, out of the blue, I "rated" one of these excuses. Exasperation was the motivation. Unintentionally, however, I was onto something: I had found a means to point out undesired behavior in a way that allowed us all to laugh at it. There is no science involved in the rating system we subsequently developed. It is totally arbitrary and also totally open to dispute by the "ratee." Late for dinner because of a flat tire? A 10, for sure. Late because you haven't finished a game of solitaire? 0, 3, or minus 4, depending on the day. Late in order to finish reading a chapter in a book? That one, I admit, was tougher to rate in a household of devoted readers.

What's important is that rating excuses opens up a humorous dialogue in place of an accusatory one. It allows us to vent our feelings and frustrations indirectly. To this day, we still rate excuses, with a 10 meaning that the accused has trumped the accuser with ironclad justification.

How in the world did we come to be so serious in the first place? Was it something we inadvertently cultivated as we summoned all our forces to action in order to accomplish something? Was playfulness driven out of us in school, in work, or under the cloak of responsibility? Somewhere, somehow, many of us have strayed way off course: we are far too prone to give uptight or even angry responses in far too many circumstances.

A few years ago, I had the good fortune to join a seminar based on Julia Cameron's book, *The Artist's Way*. In this "spiritual workshop aimed at freeing people's creativity," we spent twelve weeks delving into various things that block and thwart personal growth and creative energies. It is interesting and significant that Cameron talks in terms of "recovery" and of re-discovering the joy and the playfulness that is so naturally present in children. I had not realized I'd lost it! How easily we are seduced into becoming practical and time-driven, focused to the point of stultifying imagination, invention, inspiration, and even basic amiability. We have to learn to "play" all over again. What's ironic is how hard it is to do that. We have to remind ourselves that while clock-watching has its place, often we carry practicality too far. We need, rather, to savor the ride—to enjoy the process, not just the product, to take pleasure in the journey, not just the destination.

Lightening up means taking things less seriously. We can unwind this predilection for practicality and prudence. We can stop drowning in a sea of weighty seriousness. Moderating intensity with lightheartedness requires concentrated effort. It takes conscious cultivation, first to recognize that the pendulum has swung too far, and then to reintroduce levity into our lives. The good news is that this is, indeed, possible. Small steps are in order: spending an hour at the piano, perhaps; experimenting with a set of paints, even—especially—if you are not a "painter"; making a soufflé, "just because"; rearranging the furniture; telling jokes; embracing silliness; enjoying small pleasures, perhaps a glass of wine, a lavender sachet, or a single rose. Once begun, lightheartedness seems to create its own forward motion, revealing possibilities, pleasures, and a sense of joy in all sorts of unexpected places.

An easygoing attitude makes magic possible. Along with re-discovered playfulness come flexibility and renewed acceptance of life with all its imperfections as well as its glories. Casting seeds of delight in a world too full of heaviness and frowns, we make the path easier, the load lighter, and the journey ever so much more satisfying.

> *A merry heart doeth good like a medicine.*
>
> —*PROVERBS 17:22*

Remember
four simple
words:
LIVE, LOVE.
LAUGH.
BLOOM.

Canon

Having the same melody throughout,
although starting at different points.

We shall not cease
from exploration
and at the end
of all our exploring
will be to arrive
where we started
and know the place
for the first time.

. T S ELIOT

Growth Is a Spiraling Process

I am more myself than I have ever been.
There is less conflict. I am happier, more balanced,
and…more powerful. I felt it is rather an odd word,
"powerful," but I think it is true. It might be more accurate
to say "I am better able to use my powers."
I am surer of what my life is about,
have less self-doubt to conquer.

—MAY SARTON

Canon: musicians' parlance for a "round," those simple melodies we learned as children and sang over and over again in endless spirals of swirling sound. Achieving balance in our lives is much like singing a round. Over and over, we experience similar situations. The trick is to recognize similarities as they are unfolding so that we can avoid kicking in with our standard default responses. Instead, we can react mindfully, making use of the lessons we learned the last time.

How many times we repeat the same lessons! Again and again, we repeat our attempts to bring the disparate issues of our lives into a workable, harmonious perspective. It seems, however, that we come out a little farther up the spiral each time. We recognize sooner that we have options that are better than that first automatic reflex, alternatives that are more appropriate and more effective. We find ourselves initiating "course corrections" that we might have been unaware of the last time around.

A few years ago, during a summertime cruise aboard our boat *Tumbleweed*, I found myself annoyed and vexed because my husband was in high gear, planning our next activity and "ignoring" my plans. Stewing privately, I suddenly realized that I had not communicated my plans. I was resenting Jack for not reading my mind. Well, I've had some laughs with women friends about this expectation being perfectly legitimate, but on a more serious note, it was eye opening to suddenly comprehend the irrationality of my behavior. I may not like to assert myself, but I can hardly hold others accountable for thoughts and wishes that I keep to myself.

Recently, another incident arose where my husband was making plans for a weekend rendezvous with old friends without my input. His assumption, which was correct, was that I would want very much to see these old friends. The problem was that I had a deadline to meet for a consulting job. My automatic reflex reaction of annoyance began to kick in but was interrupted when I remembered the cruising incident. I realized that Jack was unaware of my deadline. I was jumping off the same cliff, that is, getting annoyed when I hadn't assumed my responsibility to communicate my parameters. I took a deep breath and told him about my time crunch. We developed alternate plans that gave me time to complete my obligation. Basically, this incident was a repeat of the cruising incident. This time, however, I saw the pattern as it was emerging and changed my behavior.

Recognizing lessons from your experiences is an indication that you're on an upward path. Each time, you spot behaviors sooner and learn to react more gracefully and effectively. Life throws curve balls and distractions all the time. It takes conscious reflection and analysis, along with frequent adaptation, to stay on course. Each experience, however, leaves you in a more knowing place. As the saying goes, "When you lose, don't lose the lesson."

Some semblance of overall balance is needed to ascend this spiral path of personal growth. Without some measure of equilibrium, it is difficult to move forward, and hard, even, to discern the path. Whenever you seriously neglect one dimension of your life, problems inevitably show up in others. If I don't exercise, I get logy, which definitely diminishes my creative edge. If I'm too busy, the muscles in my neck and shoulders constrict. If I'm not getting enough quiet time, I become almost manic. If I get too pre-occupied with work projects, my social interactions suffer. Striving for balance requires regular review of how you are spending your time and an analysis of your priorities.

Balancing spontaneity and planning is an ongoing dance, a sashaying back and forth that calls for constant choreography. You have to make time for the big things first, lest they be squeezed to the sidelines by countless little things.

Some people have the ability to arrive at their balance point with remarkable spontaneity or intuition. Many of us, however, need to plan how we spend our time and schedule the "chunks." Over-planning is as big a trap as not planning at all, because it leaves no room for the unexpected, for serendipity. We've all had those weeks when every moment was spoken for and an opportunity to do something special came along. When we have over-planned, we have boxed ourselves in to a place where rearranging commitments isn't possible because there are no more hours to be arranged—period.

At the base of the spiral of growth is a wellspring that leads to balance and harmony: a deep-within place that is filled with the essence of our true, integral selves. This wellspring needs replenishing. When it runs dry, we falter. For each of us, this renewal, this personal formula for "refilling the well" is unique. There is no substitute, however, for discovering what it is that replenishes us and honoring that need. Music, nature, my journal, and my friends are the waters in my well, my oases when I'm in a desert. Knowing this about myself, I must be careful not to short-change these things when "important" matters tempt me to sideline them. These are the "sparkles" that keep me going, soothe my vulnerabilities, and restore my equanimity.

I used to think that rest and sleep were optional when life offered more exciting opportunities. I no longer think so. Nothing, absolutely nothing, is more damaging to outlook and ability to cope, let alone grow, than being overtired. Objectivity, joy, flexibility, creativity, positive attitude, generosity—all those attributes of our very best selves—fly out the window when we are exhausted, leaving us not only dangerously vulnerable but with personalities we hardly recognize, let alone like! If we would grow, we must honor the need for adequate sleep and rest. Something happens in "down time" that can't be gotten any other way.

Finally comes our forever friend: attitude. We cannot choose what happens to us, but we can choose our attitudes. We can choose to be thankful. We can choose to be glad that there is still learning to do, still discoveries to be made. We can choose to have the eyes of detectives, looking for the good in situations and grateful to have coping tools we can apply creatively. In those beautiful words from "Desiderata" by Max Ehrmann, we can choose "beyond a wholesome discipline," to be "gentle with ourselves." We can remember that we don't need to be perfect. We just need to stay in the game and continue to ascend the widening spiral of growth.

If we apply and re-apply these strategies tenaciously, again and again, we will work our way up the spiral, "singing our best songs" in an endless canon. We will rediscover those genuine selves that are so carefully buried inside us. We will learn to be those selves with greater consistency. Indeed, as Octavio Paz intimates, we—the real women God intended us to be—will, "beyond ourselves, somewhere, arrive."

> *I shall become a master in this art*
> *only after a great deal of practice.*
> —ERICH FROMM

"...it is the song from within
That keeps the pain of living
from snuffing our Lives."
MARK NEPO

Excerpted from *The Book of Awakening* by Mark Nepo.

Coda

*A section of a composition
which is added to the form proper
as a conclusion.*

'Tis Grace
hath brought me safe
Thus far; and
Grace will
lead me home.

Good Enough
Is Good Enough

...the ability to accept partial success as a reason
for contentment—after exhausting one's best efforts—
can be an enormous advantage.
—GAIL SHEEHY, *PATHFINDERS*

There you have it, a flurry of metaphors: florid "melodies," spare "bass lines," "leitmotifs," compositional strategies, the timbres of all sorts of different "instruments," all representing the tangled, complex, complicated mazes and circumstances that are the life of a woman. The lot of them form a dogged, determined collection of ideas designed to help us forge harmony and balance out of our choices as women in modern life.

My mother, my wonderful, wise mother (who lived to celebrate her ninety-eighth birthday), always maintained that everyone has problems. Wealth, popularity, brains, social stature: none of these immunize us from the pain of problems; they merely determine what kinds of problems we will have. Whether spawned by economic expediencies or an identity crisis, the problems we all face are equally real and equally painful. Indeed, our painful experiences are the harbingers of our growth, of humility, empathy, and humanity. Mother further submitted that we get sent our particular set of problems because, like an individualized curriculum, they will teach us what we need to learn.

Womansong grew out of my need for a springboard to self-discovery and self-evaluation. Combining inspirations from many disciplines and many ways of knowing allowed my fledgling sense of self-acceptance to emerge and, blessedly, to grow. Ideas empowered solutions.

Throughout history, we women have struggled to find ways to circumvent social imperatives and work within patriarchal systems in order to follow our hearts and our intuition. The nature of those struggles varies from age to age, but struggles they are, have been, and perhaps always will be. Men, of course, have their own unique crosses to bear, but in these pages I am addressing the struggles that seem especially "feminine."

How is it different these days than it was when I came through young adulthood? Surely, more choices exist for women today. Choice is a blessing, but it is also a burden, potentially making it harder to decide what to do. For instance, few young women today would think that the ministry is off limits to them. For me, it was one less possibility and so far out of reach that it didn't even figure on a list of "maybes." My daughter's list of "maybes," however, overwhelms her with its dizzying array of possibilities. She starts with virtually nothing eliminated. Locations, job descriptions, living arrangements: there are no rules and few guidelines. That's amazing, wonderful, yet also potentially paralyzing. Open-endedness is as challenging as restriction. Our daughters need tools of self-knowledge as badly as we needed them, but for different reasons. How else can they begin to make choices that are inherently compatible with who they are?

So far, the emerging social construct has failed to generate any prevalence of work schedules that are family-friendly. Many young women today are not much farther ahead than I was thirty years ago in their effort to figure out how to have an outside job and still have time for a family and a life. What does offer hope is a sense that today's young women seem less angst-ridden and more assertive. There is a sense of entitlement about being women, being feminine—no apologies needed. It took decades for many of us in my generation to deal with our angst, first to recognize this malaise for what it was and then to find ways to neutralize it. Ever so slowly, we became empowered to find the small, everyday solutions that brought us a sense of some degree of rightness with the world. Our daughters seem to have more inherent respect for their own worth.

Somehow, women—all of us, any age—need to refine our definition of success. Success does not mean absolute, complete perfection. We'll never be perfect, but we can be "good enough." If we can be good enough, we no longer need to be hypercritical and hyper-needy. We are what we are, each of us a total discrete package with some good traits and some that are less than admirable. My friend Marsha puts it so beautifully, "I'm not perfect, but parts of me are excellent!" We are unfinished products striving for wholeness. We need each other, too, because we won't find wholeness hidden behind a Maginot Line of isolation and deception.

Women have gigantic hurdles to surmount in today's society, but we often forget our greatest assets and our most potent, powerful weapons: each other. Ironically, when we doubt ourselves and each other, we aid and abet all those forces that prevent our progress. While there is no one, tidy Grand Solution to overcoming very real societal obstacles and difficult problems, our first line of defense—and offense—should be to turn to each other. The first order of business needs to be listening to each other. We assume we know what other women think, but there are so many variations on this feminine theme! Listening and talking, laughing and crying, we need to be brave enough and trusting enough to hear and to honor each others' truths.

For the most part, even when we women are a mess inside, we put out very "together" impressions. However, letting down your guard allows mutual trust to blossom. Taking the risk of allowing yourself to be vulnerable by summoning the nerve to confide in other women and listening to their responses and opinions is incredibly empowering. Without exception, my efforts to share problems and quandaries with other women have resulted in enormous support, empathy, clarity, generosity, and friendship. Until you share your thoughts, it's easy for your friends, who suffer from their own vulnerabilities and insecurities, to think you couldn't possibly understand theirs.

There is a sublime fellowship, an uncanny, intuitive connection, among women who dare to uncover this vast reservoir by opening themselves to their sisters. We see the power of the "old boys' network," and at times we begrudge it, yet we often fail to capitalize on our own empathic, nurturing skills by creating uniquely feminine networks that are strong, comforting, and effective. Unsure of our own worth, we put down the choices other women make to affirm our own. It's the "If I belittle your choices, somehow I make mine look better," argument. How sad.

When we stop thinking we alone have the One True Answer, we might just begin to be on the track of true success. True success does not judge; it quietly accomplishes what it can, where it can, thankful for each day of opportunities. It allows us to begin to cultivate the pleasure of little triumphs, small gains, and joy in little things. In *The Bone People*, Keri Hulme observes, "a man can find satisfaction with enough." So must we all.

I do not mean to imply any sexist agenda through these deliberations about complicated issues with deeply entrenched male versus female overtones. The flux in gender roles is a huge conundrum for men as well as for women. Their traditional roles have been assailed, criticized, downplayed, and attacked with mesmerizing fury which must leave reasonable men wondering what in the world they are supposed to do. Nonetheless, certainly men have uniquely male ways of being and ways of interrelating. We need to recognize, even celebrate, the differences in male and female styles and rhythms. Our mistake is trying to adapt to modes that are not inherent in our nature, the masculine yang instead of our feminine yin; their "animus" ways instead of our "anima" ways. We must learn to use well whatever strengths have been given us, including any uniquely feminine attributes.

We need to be willing to look beyond the obvious and realize that often things are not what they seem. People who exude confidence (as I did) may be filled with self-doubt. People who are indefatigably cheerful may be valiantly railing against private sorrow. Other people's experiences can be touchstones for our own discoveries if we are able to set aside our judgments and preconceived notions. We need to be sure enough of our own inherent worth to put aside the temptation to belittle others.

Our unresolved issues, whatever they are, dictate our personal lesson plans in life. Whether it is pain within our minds or pain "without," in the world, no one brand of problems is more or less than another; it is just different. For the most part, my personal issues have been theoretical ones. I find myself mysteriously compelled to think, always think, driven by the compulsion that if I think hard enough, I will understand, and that if I understand, I will therefore be able to create solutions. "Understanding everything changes nothing," my friend Marsha reminds me. My "curriculum" has been to learn to accept what is, to influence what is changeable, and to find serenity somehow, somewhere, within life's confusing contradictions.

Each of us, then, has a unique destiny, a journey toward balance and harmony as individual as we ourselves are. There will be obstacles but also serendipities; heartaches but also joys; predictable phases but also surprising turns in the road. Our job is to pay attention, to be open, to learn, and to love. Oh, yes—and to be flexible! The final talisman for learning to sing our personal, inborn song comes from the classic children's book *Daddy-Long-Legs*:

> *The world is full of happiness,*
> *and plenty to go around, if you are*
> *only willing to take the kind that comes your way.*
> *The whole secret is being pliable.*
>
> —JEAN WEBSTER

Expect a lag
between
letting go
of the person
you were
and
getting used
to the person
you are becoming

Muses

Guiding spirits, sources of inspiration.

As the sun illuminates
the moon and the stars
so let us illumine each other.

Suggested Readings

I suggest that the only books that influence us
are those for which we are ready, and which have gone
a little farther down our own particular path
than we have yet got ourselves.

—E. M. FORSTER

Books have been my trusted friends since I was a small child. Certainly there are many, many books that address the issues of woman's identity in a changing world. The following are a few that have been most meaningful or helpful to me personally in my quest for self-discovery.

WHAT'S THE PROBLEM?

Orenstein, Peggy. *Flux: Women on Sex, Work, Love, Kids, and Life in a Half-Changed World.* New York: Doubleday, 2000. *The title says it all. This book articulates the conundrums of changing gender roles and cultural expectations.*

UNDERSTANDING THE SOCIAL AND CULTURAL BACKGROUND

Brooks, David. *Bobos in Paradise: The New Upper Class and How They Got There.* New York: Simon & Schuster, 2000. *Bobos is a lively social commentary about a newly amalgamated class emerging in America. Bobos mix bourgeois and bohemian values and ideologies that formerly were distinctly separate. Highly entertaining, this book is also a powerful critique of the current socio-cultural climate in America.*

Brooks, David. *On Paradise Drive: How We Live Now (And Always Have) in the Future Tense.* New York: Simon & Schuster, 2004. *What does it mean to be American? Hilarious, insightful—inciteful—look at how future-mindedness influences American culture.*

Ehrenreich, Barbara. *Fear of Falling: The Inner Life of the Middle Class.* New York: Random House, 1989. *We think we control our ideas and outlooks, but actually these things are greatly influenced by the social milieu that surrounds us. In the case of the vast middle class, there is more angst about maintaining that status than most of us realize. A fascinating study of contemporary American sub-cultures.*

Koontz, Stephanie. *The Way We Never Were: American Families and The Nostalgia Trap.* New York: Basic Books, 1992. *A lively discussion that separates fact from fiction and shatters myths and half-truths about family life in America. "Placing current family dilemmas in the context of far-reaching economic, political, and demographic changes, Stephanie Koontz sheds new light on such contemporary concerns as parenting, privacy, love, the division of labor along gender lines, the black family, feminism, and sexual practice."*

Mintz, Steven, and Kellogg, Susan. *Domestic Revolutions: A Social History of American Family Life.* New York: The Free Press, 1988. *What are families in America? How did they evolve? How does where we've been relate to where we're going? This historical overview analyzes the hows and whys of family life from the Colonial era until the 1980s.*

Sheehy, Gail. *New Passages: Mapping Your Life Across Time.* New York: Random House, 1995. *A breakthrough book that describes the stages of adulthood, including the predictable outlooks, conflicts, and crises that occur in each phase. Indispensable for understanding what's going on in your own life and in the lives of those you love, not to mention those who are hard to love but whom you must deal with, anyway!*

Sheehy, Gail. *Pathfinders: Overcoming the Crises of Adult Life and Finding Your Own Path.* New York: William Morrow, 1981. *Dated; but personally, reading this book was a seminal experience. Taking in the stories of how actual people dealt with adult passages and found ways to accomplish their goals was a turning point, helping me to figure out what I had to do to get going with my life.*

Sulloway, Frank J. *Born to Rebel: Birth Order, Family Dynamics and Creative Lives.* New York: Pantheon, 1996. *When it comes to how we view ourselves and the world, birth order may have more to do with it than we ever realized. Sulloway's scholarly yet extremely readable book brings an entirely new dimension to thinking about what forms us and how to understand complicated relationships within families.*

VARIATIONS ON THE THEME:
WOMEN (AND ONE MAN) THINKING ABOUT WOMANHOOD

Bateson, Mary Catherine. *Composing a Life.* New York: Plume, 1989.
*These interwoven, comparative biographies of five professional women
serve as a platform for considering our own choices.*
French, Marilyn. *The Bleeding Heart.* New York: Ballentine, 1980.
French, Marilyn. *Her Mother's Daughter.* New York: Ballentine, 1987.
French, Marilyn. *Our Father.* London: Hamish Hamilton, 1994.
French, Marilyn. *The Women's Room.* New York: Jove, 1977.
*Marilyn French has an extraordinary talent for winding a story around
women's issues as a means of helping us to think about them. Each of
these tales examines various aspects of being a wife, mother, lover, or
daughter and leaves us in a different place. Her Mother's Daughter
stands out for setting up a story with gender role reversals that force the
reader to examine his or her own biases.*
Heilbrun, Carolyn G. *The Last Gift of Time: Life Beyond Sixty.* New York,
Ballentine, 1997.
Heilbrun, Carolyn G. *Reinventing Womanhood.* New York: Norton, 1979.
Heilbrun, Carolyn G. *Writing a Woman's Life.* New York: Norton, 1988.
*As one reads her memoirs, Heilbrun comes to feel like an old friend. Her
musings illuminate women's questions, heartaches, and conundrums with
light, humor, and fresh air.*
L'Engle, Madeleine. *A Circle of Quiet.* San Francisco: Harper. Reissue
edition, 1984. *This journal shares fruitful reflections on life and career
prompted by the author's visit to her personal place of retreat near
her country home. Jean Kerr says it best: "My favorite of all Madeleine
L'Engle's books. Lovely, charming, a book to cherish. I know it will give
great consolation to ordinary people who sometimes wonder why they
bother to get out of bed in the morning."*
Shields, Carol. *Small Ceremonies.* Toronto: Vintage Canada, 1976.
Shields, Carol. *The Stone Diaries.* New York: Penguin, 1993.
*Women, their lives, their ideas—more rich food for thought about how women
lead their lives.*
Tyler, Anne. *Ladder of Years.* New York: Knopf, 1995. *Tyler's books are full
of ordinary women struggling with ordinary issues. This story deals with
responsibility. Tyler presents the provocative idea that sometimes respon-*

sibility is like an object on a table, and it is for us to decide whether or not to pick it up.

Wilber, Ken. *Grace and Grit: Spirituality and Healing in the Life and Death of Treya Killam Wilber.* Boston: Shambala, 1993. *This is actually a love story, a brave account of one woman's experience with breast cancer. Central to Treya's struggles, however, beyond the cancer, was the issue of doing versus being, an important question in the search for one's individual identity.*

POSSIBILITIES

Cardozo, Arlene Rossen. *Sequencing: A New Solution for Women Who Want Marriage, Career, and Family.* New York: Collier, 1986. *This is the so-called "mommy track" book. Considering this option is one more way of figuring out who you really are, what you really want, and what the possibilities really are.*

Friedan, Betty. *The Fountain of Age.* New York: Simon and Schuster, 1993. *A wonderful, singular book full of possibilities and ideas for aging. Friedan offers many new ways to think about and deal with growing older.*

Godfrey, Joline. *Our Wildest Dreams: Women Entrepreneurs Making Money, Having Fun, Doing Good.* New York: Harper Business, 1992. *Actual accounts of women who started their own businesses, made their own rules, and succeeded in an economy dominated by the old (male) paradigm. (It's not about male bashing; it is just very exciting and inspiring. It can be done!)*

Hochschild, Arlie Russell with Machung, Anne. *The Second Shift.* Second Edition. New York: Penguin Books, 2003. *A searing analysis of the human impact of two-career families.*

Hochschild, Arlie Russell. *Time Bind: When Work Becomes Home & Home Becomes Work.* New York: Metropolitan, 1997. *Consideration of the important questions about how we spend our time and how we prioritize and the possible implications and alternatives.*

THINKING ABOUT MARRIAGE

Carter, Betty, and Peters, Joan K. *Love, Honor, and Negotiate: Building Partnerships that Last a Lifetime.* New York: Pocket Books, 1996. *An enormously* helpful discussion of how marriage "contracts" evolve and how couples can learn to communicate and negotiate effectively to enhance concurrently both their relationship and their individual interests. Easily and by far the single best book I have read about making a marriage work.

Heyn, Dalma. *Marriage Shock: The Transformation of Women into Wives.* New York: Villard, 1997. This wonderful, unsung book examines how women unconsciously weave cultural expectations into their marriages and then wonder what happened to them. By advocating the realization of full potential for both partners, Heyn's book is pro-marriage in a most positive, healthy way.

Viorst, Judith. *Grown-up Marriage: What We Know, Wish We Had Known, and Still Need to Know about Being Married.* New York: Free Press, 2003. "Life-affirming book on the difficulties and possibilities of being well and enduringly wed." Like all of Viorst's books, this one is highly readable and engaging.

Wallerstein, Judith S., and Blakeslee, Sandra. *The Good Marriage: How and Why Love Lasts.* New York: Houghton Mifflin, 1995. A discussion of the types and natural stages of marriage. Compelling explanation of psychological tasks that must be undertaken by anyone committed to having a good marriage. "Wise, original insights of the many, many roads to marital happiness."

THINKING ABOUT MOTHERHOOD

Crittenden, Ann. *The Price of Motherhood: Why the Most Important Job in the World Is Still the Least Valued.* New York: Henry Holt, 2001. Disturbing, discouraging, important, and necessary! Crittenden spells out the problems, and we won't solve them until we face them.

Mahony, Rhona. *Kidding Ourselves: Breadwinning, Babies, and Bargaining Power.* New York: Basic Books, 1995. "...full of important insights about why 'women's work' remains just that and what women can do to change it."

Marshall, Melinda M. *Good Enough Mothers: Changing Expectations for Ourselves.* Princeton: Peterson's, 1993. Marshall recognizes that the resolutions to our views of "good enough" lie within. She presents multiple sides of multiple issues, case studies, and thoughts about arriving at workable compromises.

O'Mara, Peggy. *A Quiet Place: Essays on Life and Family.* Santa Fe: Mothering Publications, 2005. *A compilation of favorite editorials from Mothering magazine. "A treasure of wisdom that will ease the hearts and minds of parents everywhere."*

Rhodes, Sonya, with Wilson, Joleen. *Surviving Family Life: The Seven Crises of Living Together.* New York: Putnam's, 1981. *I returned to this book again and again over twenty years of parenthood as I struggled to grow into each new phase. This is a valuable resource when struggling for intergenerational perspective.*

Roiphe, Anne. *Fruitful: A Real Mother in the Modern World.* Boston: Houghton Mifflin, 1996. *First-person account of a woman's journey through the second half of the twentieth century. Roiphe talks about guilt, feminism, the nuclear family, values, fatherhood, and much more. Rich food for thought.*

BASICS: A PERSONAL TAKE ON THE BEST OF THE "KNOW THYSELF" GENRE

Boffey, D. Barnes. *Reinventing Yourself: A Control Theory Approach to Becoming the Person You Want to Be.* Chapel Hill: New View Publications, 1993. *Further expounds on Control Theory, (see Good, E. Perry, below) with specific suggestions about using the concepts to break away from old, outgrown, or destructive patterns and create new, enabling habits.*

Bolen, Jean Shinoda, M.D. *Crones Don't Whine: Concentrated Wisdom for Juicy Women.* San Francisco: Conari Press, 2003. *Don't be put off by the word "crone"—this is a little book with thirteen light-hearted essays about qualities all women will want to cultivate.*

Canfield, Jack, and Hansen, Mark Victor. *The Aladdin Factor.* New York: Berkeley Books, 1995. *It seems people either feel free to ask anyone and everyone for everything without discrimination or hesitation, or they figure they need to do everything for themselves. As someone in the latter category, reading this book changed my life by showing me how to ask for what I want.*

Good, E. Perry. *In Pursuit of Happiness: Knowing What You Want, Getting What You Need.* Chapel Hill: New View Publications, 1987. *Control Theory—the idea that all people have a psychological need for love,*

power, fun, and freedom—offers a useful framework for considering personal progress in achieving goals. Understanding underlying motivation
helps to reveal proactive possibilities for making our dreams become
reality. Easy to read, great graphics, targeted exercises.

Lerner, Harriet Goldhor. *The Dance of Anger: A Woman's Guide to Changing the Patterns of Intimate Relationships.* New York: Harper & Row,
1985. We've all been there: angry as hell and trying to deny it rather
than deal with it. This is the book that "shows women how to turn anger
into a constructive force for reshaping their lives." A book that should be
on every woman's bookshelf as a ready reference when one is ambushed
by anger.

Lerner, Harriet Goldhor. *Fear and Other Uninvited Guests: Tackling the
Anxiety, Fear, and Shame That Keep Us from Optimal Living and Loving.* New York: Harper Collins, 2004. If you've ever been paralyzed by
fear, it's good to have a source of objective thinking about how you can
deal with it. Straightforward, easy to read, helpful.

Lindbergh, Reeve. *Forward From Here: Leaving Middle Age—and Other
Unexpected Adventures.* New York: Simon & Schuster, 2008. Reflections on aging. "Time flies," says Lindbergh. "but if I am willing to fly with
it, then I can be airborne, too." Gentle, humorous, insightful.

Luskin, Dr. Fred. *Forgive for Good: A Proven Prescription for Health and
Happiness.* New York: Harper Collins San Francisco, 2002. An examination of grievance and forgiveness, with techniques and methods for
getting unstuck when you find yourself locked in a state of being unable
to forgive and move on. Very useful.

Pipher, Mary. *Seeking Peace: Chronicles of the Worst Buddhist in the World.*
New York: Riverhead Books, 2009. In this thoughtful and inspiring
memoir, the author of Reviving Ophelia explores her personal search
for understanding, tranquility, and respect. Pipher's experiences—while
unique—are somehow very familiar and most encouraging. A gem for
those of us who are hard on ourselves.

Quindlen, Anna. *Being Perfect.* New York: Random House, 2005. Avoiding
the "perfection trap," a spot-on essay by an incomparable contemporary
author and journalist.

Sewell, Marilyn, ed. *Breaking Free: Women of Spirit at Midlife and Beyond.*
Boston: Beacon Press, 2004. Twenty-seven essays by famous women of

our time grappling with what age has taught them. A poignant collection about losses, gains, lessons, and yes, "breaking free."

Thoele, Sue Patton. *The Mindful Woman: Gentle Practices for Restoring Calm, Finding Balance & Opening Your Heart.* Oakland: New Harbinger Publications, 2008. Simple and effective practices for learning to live in the moment and quiet the mind.

Viorst, Judith. *Imperfect Control: Our Lifelong Struggles with Power and Surrender.* New York: Fireside, 1999. "Whose life is not impacted, if not defined, by issues of control?" Viorst "shows us how our sense of self and all our important relationships are colored by our struggles over control: over wanting it and taking it, loving it and fearing it, and figuring out when the time has come to surrender it."

Viorst, Judith. *Necessary Losses: The Loves, Illusions, Dependencies and Impossible Expectations That All of Us Have to Give Up in Order to Grow.* New York: Fawcett Gold Medal, 1986. Losses: It is tempting to try to prevent them or to deny them, but the truth is, they are necessary. "Conversational, not clinical." Viorst examines the nature of the various kinds of loss and coaxes us to embrace them and learn to move on.

MOTHERS AND DAUGHTERS

Northrup, Christane, M.D. *Mother-Daughter Wisdom: Creating a Legacy of Physical and Emotional Help.* New York: Bantam Dell, 2006. A book that helps us "get clear about the ways in which our mother's history both influenced and continues to inform our state of health, our beliefs, and how we live our lives." Useful combination of science, reason, history, and heart.

Roberts, Cokie. *We Are Our Mothers' Daughters.* New York: William Morrow, 2009. "…a fine vehicle for discussion or individual contemplation, giving both mothers and daughters new perspectives for viewing one another."

Stoddard, Alexandra. *Things I Want My Daughters to Know: A Small Book about the Big Issues in Life.* New York: HarperCollins, 2004. Ironically, this is the book I thought I was trying to write when I started to work on Womansong. Provides tidy, positive, pro-active observations on issues that influence the quality of our lives.

Stoddard, Alexandra. *Things Good Mothers Know.* New York: HarperCollins, 2009. *A lovely, warm, wise book of little essays about motherhood, reminding us of the things we (mostly) know but often forget.*

THE CRÈME DE LA CRÈME: MOTHER LODE OF INSPIRATION

Gibran, Kahlil. *The Prophet.* New York: Alfred A. Knopf, 1961. *Gibran's masterpiece. Here are spiritual musings on the central themes of human life. "Cadenced and vibrant with feeling, the words of Kahlil Gibran bring to one's ears the majestic rhythm of Ecclesiastes."*

Hammarskjöld, Dag. *Markings.* New York: Alfred A. Knopf, 1965. *Hammarskjöld described his writings as a "sort of white book concerning my negotiations with myself and with God." Most entries are short poems or a sentence or two—pithy phrases that speak with wisdom about common situations, problems, and anxieties. A treasure.*

Lindbergh, Anne Morrow. *Gift from the Sea.* New York: Pantheon, 1955. *An exquisite meditation on women's lives and values, based on seashell metaphors. I read this yearly, and it speaks to me differently each time.*

Palmer, Parker J. *A Hidden Wholeness: The Journey Toward An Undivided Life.* San Francisco: Jossey-Bass, 2004. *One senses an authenticity in Palmer's musings that makes his voice compelling and awesome. He theorizes that we are born "whole" but forget somewhere along the way who we really are. This book is devoted to figuring out how to live "divided no more."*

Palmer, Parker J. *The Courage to Teach: Exploring the Inner Landscape of a Teacher's Life.* San Francisco: Jossey-Bass, 1998. *Ostensibly a book about teachers and teaching, Palmer's book moved me with its intensely spiritual message to be authentic—whatever we do.*

Williamson, Marianne. *A Woman's Worth.* New York: Random House, 1993. *A beautiful "little book" that reminds women of who they are and inspires them to get beyond stereotypes and media messages to self-realization.*

COMMUNICATION

Fisher, Roger, and Ury, William. *Getting to Yes: Negotiating Agreement without Giving In.* New York: Penguin Books, 1981. *Based on the*

Harvard Negotiation Project, this book outlines the personal version of "win-win" or interest-based negotiation, a major tool of effective personal communication. Very highly recommended!

Gilligan, Carol. *In a Different Voice: Psychological Theory and Women's Development.* Cambridge: Harvard University Press, 1982. *Gilligan shows that conventional psychological theory has been based on the observations of men's lives, implying that "normal" is the male way of doing things. She begins the discussion of looking at behavior with a new set of parameters, that of women. Fascinating, liberating.*

Tannen, Deborah. *You Just Don't Understand: Women and Men in Conversation.* New York: Ballentine Books, 1990. *An essential book for understanding the differences in method, nuance, and meaning in how men and women communicate. Very helpful in learning to "speak the other's language," or at least to interpret what is being said!*

LIVING CREATIVELY

Beck, Martha. *Finding Your Own North Star: Claiming the Life You Were Meant to Live.* New York: Three Rivers Press, 2001. *Useful, extremely accessible ideas about reconnecting with our essential selves. Includes exercises to aid the process of self-discovery and self-affirmation.*

Cameron, Julia. *The Artist's Way: A Spiritual Path to Higher Creativity.* New York: Penguin Putnam, 1992. *We live in a left-brain dominant world, full of facts, necessities, schedules, and limits. Cameron dares us to look at life differently: to play, to honor creativity, and to be open to synchronicities and serendipities. Following her twelve-week course will change your life—guaranteed!*

Digh, Patti: *Life is a Verb: 37 Ways to Wake up, Be Mindful, and Live Intentionally.* Guilford: Skirt!, 2008. *Unusual, colorful book chock full of ideas, challenges, suggested actions and core practices for living life without regrets.*

IN A CLASS BY THEMSELVES

Angier, Natalie. *Woman: An Intimate Geography.* New York: Anchor Books, 1999. *Truly unique! Angier has the soul of a poet and the mind of a sci-*

entist, and she brings both of those to bear on the subject of the biology and evolution of woman. Fascinating, captivating, dazzling—a must-read for anyone interested in womanhood.

Borysenko, Joan, Ph.D. *A Woman's Book of Life: The Biology, Psychology, and Spirituality of the Feminine Life Cycle.* New York: Riverhead Books, 1996. A beautiful, inspiring, uplifting book that shows how the various dimensions of women interact and relate to form the whole person. Provides excellent chapters on how childhood experiences influence later life, and on menopause. Highest recommendation!

Taylor, Barbara Brown. *An Altar in the World: A Geography of Faith.* New York: Harper One, 2009. Yes, it's about religion...but it so much more— a book about the many dimensions of each person, about acceptance, compassion, and balance. A treasure!

Acknowledgments

I am a part of all whom I have met, and if I have any success, it is because the goodness and love of my family and friends have made it possible.

Renée Locks, her generosity and openness to a "call from the Universe" stands out as one of the miracles in my life.

My father, **August von der Osten**, a man with foresight, insight, and uncompromising sense of excellence.

My mother, **Louise Fellows von der Osten,** indefatigably optimistic, an inspired "Dorothea" and the best role model possible! Mother never judged; she was always willing to give others the benefit of doubt. Her cup was never half-empty, always half-full, a legacy she imparted to me.

My daughter, **Jennifer Suesse Stine,** one of my best teachers, my peerless friend, and the source of many of my quotes and ideas.

My son, **Ned Suesse,** who lightens me up with his flexibility and humor, has guided me in the "book business," and whose knack for metaphorical thinking has influenced my writing.

My mother-in-law, **Margaret Frank Suesse,** whose pluck in the face of adversity is an inspiration to all who know her.

My sisters, **Barbara Kroger** and **Marjorie Metzler,** and my women friends, always there with a shoulder, a smile, a piece of chocolate or advice, and ready to share through thick and thin. Life without my buddies is truly unimaginable.

Peggy Hanousek, mentor and friend. She was the first to read the entire first draft and help me know how to continue.

Jean Wright, who first suggested framing this book in musical terms. I have counted on her incisive eye, her spot-on critiques, and her endless encouragement.

Marsha Van Hecke, Kindred Spirit, trusted friend, sister writer, savvy proofreader, and indefatigable supporter—be it with kindness, an understanding ear, a glass of wine, or simple "presence."

Susan Beardslee, Laurie Carlson, Merilyn Field, Corinne Fuller, Linda Haynes, Mary Clare Jenks, Rita Landrum, Marcia Madden, Edith McConnell, Margaret Allen Marshall, Ouida Spalding, Kathy Willis, and **Peggy Zimmerman,** each of whom influenced this book in some pivotal way.

My colleagues at the Displaced Homemaker Program in Syracuse, NY, from whom I learned so much, and with whom I had so much fun.

Peggy Millin, Virginia McCullough, and **Sarah Aschenbach,** editors and writing coaches. Their observations helped me pull my reflections together and find an appropriate structure for them. Without their input, *Womansong* would be languishing somewhere in limbo.

Most of all, my beloved late husband, **Jack.** None of this could have come about without his unquestioning faith in me and his unselfish support. He was the best!

Incalzando

Pressing forward.